RUNNING
A LIBRARY

RUNNING A LIBRARY

Managing the Congregation's
Library with Care, Confidence,
and Common Sense

RUTH S. SMITH

The Seabury Press · New York

1982
The Seabury Press
815 Second Avenue
New York, N.Y. 10017

Printed in the United States of America

Library of Congress Cataloging in Publication Data

Smith, Ruth S.
    Running a library.
    Bibliography: p.119
1. Libraries, Church—Administration.   2. Synagogue
libraries—Administration.   I. Title.
Z675.C5S53   027.6'7   82-5784
ISBN 0-8164-2413-6   AACR2

This book was written in cooperation with the Church and Synagogue
Library Association, P.O. Box 1130 Bryn Mawr, Pa. 19010.

Grateful acknowledgement is made for the use of the following
materials:

"Hints from Heloise," copyright King Features Syndicate, Inc., New York, N.Y.

"Reader Suggests Forms for Circulation Records," by Mrs. Robert Kennedy,
Grand Rapids, Michigan, *Lutheran Libraries*, V6, M1, Fall, 1963. A
publication of the Lutheran Church Library Association, Minneapolis,
Minnesota.

CONTENTS

PREFACE

Topics such as insurance, fire damage, and silverfish might have been mentioned in my classes in library school, but they were long since forgotten by the time I faced my first real-life library management assignment. The practical business of running a library—dealing with people, obtaining funding, moving the collection from place to place—had to be learned on the job.

Each library is a little different, but basic principles of administration remain the same. Over the years I have assembled certain rules of thumb and other thoughts that proved to be successful for me. I hope they may be helpful to others.

My first discovery was that the nitty-gritty requirements of library management can be more fun if you approach them as elements in a game. All the challenges are there—hazards, reversals, advances, or successes—to be avoided, accepted, or met head on. The better you know how to play the game, the better you are able to turn even the reverses to some advantage in achieving the ultimate goal of an effective library ministry.

Like any other game, library administration has rules. A primary rule is to learn the accepted procedures for operating within your own organization. For example, find out where you fit and what responsibilities you really have. Be businesslike and find out how to get things done. Develop specific guidelines for the necessary activities of budgeting, ordering, and record-keeping. In coping with crises, such as fire, theft, or water damage, ask the advice of others who have handled similar problems successfully and use your own ingenuity. Learn enough about standard library practices, such as cataloging, circulating and storing materials, to be able to teach others to help.

This book is intended to aid and inspire church and synagogue librarians, chairmen of library committees, pastors, or others who are in a position to manage programs and resources for the congregation. I hope it will demonstrate the effectiveness of a positive and optimistic approach to the unique administrative problems of a library or multimedia learning resources center.

The techniques and examples were gathered over a decade of working with volunteers, teaching workshop classes, corresponding and talking with librarians in public, school, and special libraries—particularly congregational libraries—around the country. Some of the material is based on my personal experience as a professional librarian and administrator of a special library for a nonprofit research organization, and as a church librarian and library committee chairman for many years—and still a volunteer worker on the staff—in the library of the Bethesda, Maryland, United Methodist Church.

I am in debt to the many people who have contributed information which was sifted and sorted to produce this book. I am also deeply grateful to my God who channels my efforts into such satisfying endeavors.

1

OPERATING WITHIN AN ORGANIZATION

The crowd of parishioners and well-wishers stood breathless. All eyes were focused on the steeple dangling precariously from the end of a crane high above the church roof. Only a short while before it had arrived on a truck. Workers had fastened ropes at just the right places and, at a signal from the leader, the hoist began. Slowly now the steeple was eased into its position atop the roof. When it was secured, the ropes were released, and the crowd cheered.

Teamwork, and a lot of advance planning, made the project run smoothly. Months in advance a great deal of effort went into drawing, estimating, budgeting, contracting, building, and finally, delivering the finished product. Many people had to assume responsibility. Each had to find out what was expected, know when it had to be done, and work with others to make the project succeed. This required organization.

Few worthwhile programs just happen. They are developed within a framework of organization and administrative leadership. Behind every creative ministry there always is a practical business side. The library is no exception.

Whether you call it a learning resource center, an information media center, or a library, there are practical managerial techniques and knowledge that will make it run more smoothly and therefore fulfill its purposes.

Dealing with the Administration

As an administrator, you will be operating within the organization of the church to get things done, working with the

1

library committee, and reaching out to the congregation. Communication (reaching out to others), confidence (knowing how things work), and enthusiasm (being sold on your mission)—tempered by a little tact and an understanding of the differences in individual personalities—are essential ingredients for gaining cooperation and support.

Reach toward others. Take the initiative. Rather than wait for others to come to you, approach them. It is a good idea, the first time, to ask their advice. Few people can resist an acknowledgment that their opinion is of worth. Generally, such an approach elicits a sympathetic response.

Recognize differences. Get to know the personalities of key people. Older members particularly often resist change. They are likely to oppose any new idea unless it is introduced to them gradually. Even then it is best if the idea is based on tradition or supports a long-standing goal of the congregation. Other people will jump aboard any new bandwagon that looks attractive and is moving, without looking carefully where it is headed. The latter, however, are likely to abandon the idea as quickly as they adopted it. Some people measure every activity against the budget and the bottom-line-dollar balance. Others will see only the shining goal to be achieved and care little about the details of practical "how to get there."

Find Where You Fit

You need to know where in the organizational structure you fit. What is the chain of command? What are the channels for action? Who are the key people in a position to get things done? Find the "power center" of the organization and learn how things work. This is not always easy. Individuals who are established in the hierarchy will not always share this kind of information with newcomers. Sometimes the "in" people form a closed club. In other cases, the people who wield the most influence do not really hold the positions of authority. No one likes to admit that the chairman holds little power and that the real voice of authority sits in the back row. What you are not able to find out from a friend, you most certainly will learn from experience.

Organizational structure. The library is part of a larger organization. Within this organization you will report to a higher authority—the pastor or the rabbi, the education committee, or possibly the administrative board. Your name on the official organization chart makes you an important part of the team. You belong.

Discover your place in the structure. Begin by drawing a simple chart with the library as the first box. To whom do you report? Draw another box above the library box and connect the two with a line. Fill in the answer in the second box. If you are not sure of the answer, consult the person who appointed you, or the pastor. After all, the pastor is an administrator too. He should know the structure of the church and, in addition, ought to be aware of your responsibilities and interest. More than that, he can help you fill in other boxes on the chart to show where the library fits into the total organization.

In a small congregation, the minister might appoint a librarian who then manages the library and reports to him. The lines of administration and communication are loose and informal. In a larger, more structured church, an administrative board controls a council on ministries, to whom a library committee reports. Then the librarian reports to the library committee.

The Library Chain of Command

When you have established your "place in the sun," announce it, but not boastfully or apologetically. Make it known through discreet announcements about the library—in the church or synagogue newsletter, the worship bulletin, and reports to special groups.

The real chain of command. Theoretically, administrative communication to and from the library flows over these connecting links and through the intervening boxes. But this is not always the way things actually work. For example, particularly in a small church, almost every idea or plan channels through the minister first, where it is either encouraged or shot down, before it is presented to the appropriate administrative bodies. If this is true for you, add another box on the chart for the minister and connect the library to it with a dotted line. Add a note at the bottom to check things out with him first.

Check with the Minister — First

As you identify the key members of the congregation, write their names beneath the boxes where they have their greatest influence. For example, if the minister's wife is active in the congregation's affairs, add her name and telephone number below the minister's box. She may turn out to be your greatest ally. A wise administrator lines up support before presenting a budget or other plan for the library. This usually ensures success.

Channels for action. Once you know where you fit in the organization, find out how your congregation as a whole conducts its business. Quite often a proposal for a new program must be approved by several bodies, not necessarily in the direct line of command. For example, a proposal which requires expenditure of funds, must channel through the Finance Committee from the Council on Ministries, before it can be taken to the Administrative Board for approval. Similarly, any request for a salaried librarian to run the library would need the approval of the group that hires the church staff, either before or after it goes through the Finance Committee.

Playing the game. Do it their way. Operate within the organizational and political structure according to internal rules that have been established. This will not inhibit creativity. Rather, it will help get your creative programs approved.

Work with a Library Committee

A library committee will help to carry information about plans and programs to and from the various activities within the congregation. Ask each group that the library hopes to serve to appoint an individual who will serve on the library committee. This is good public relations as well.

The Washington, D.C., Hebrew Congregation Library is managed by a volunteer committee appointed by the President of the Congregation upon recommendation of the Executive Director and/or the Committee Chairman; the Chairman reports informally to the congregation at its annual membership meeting.[1]

Not every library needs an organized committee to look after its interests and communicate with its users. In a small congregation, the librarian might well manage these things alone—at least until the library or the congregation grows to the size where more help is needed to establish goals and administer the library programs.

Policy statements. It is wise to begin with a statement of purpose. Put it in writing and post it for all to see. Some libraries add rules about the use of the library. Here are two examples of policy statements:

> The Memorial Library in Bethesda was established by the United Church in 1956. Its purpose is to provide information and resource materials, as a ministry to the pastor, to the church school and other activities of the church, and to individual parishioners, both adults and children, in support of the overall goals and objectives of the church.

> The library, supported by the Council of Ministries, is a special collection of resource material to support the programs of the _____ Church and to encourage development of Christian living. The library is open for use whenever the church is open. Rules for borrowing are posted. The librarian and/or a member of the library staff will be on duty each Sunday between the worship services to help find material or to answer questions.

Another useful policy statement that should be put into writing is the criteria for selecting resources. Example:

> Material selected for the Information Media Center must be current, authoritative, and attractive. It should reflect the needs of the congregation—the ministerial staff, the lay leadership and individual parishoners— for information and inspiration. For these purposes, it may contain any resources deemed necessary to carry on the work of the church. In general, the subjects and formats will reflect current program needs rather than archival interests.

All policies should reflect the needs and personality of the congregation. For example, Carl Weller looks for books his constituency will be interested in. He says, "The topic should be of current interest, the book well-written, and not offensive to members of the _____ Church."[2]

Administrative Tips

In summary, a good administrator will know how to operate within the organization the library serves, be able to get along well with people, and take a leadership role in helping to provide an effective library ministry. To this I would add, make God your partner. Ask him for guidance and be willing to follow his lead.

> Oh, Lord, I could never do these things without you. I give myself and the library to you. Allow me to be your humble administrator and receive your glorious plans into my heart and mind. Show me the way you would have the library grow and prosper. Together— thy will be done. Amen.

2

BUDGETING FOR GROWTH

"Dad, I need ten dollars."

"What do you need it for?"

"Oh, some things I want to get."

"No."

"But, dad, I really need the money."

"You should learn to budget your allowance better."

The word "budget" has a negative connotation for many people. It says "hold back," "don't spend," "sacrifice." Actually, quite the contrary is true. Budgeting means planning ahead, so you will have funds to cover the things you really want or need. For example, the above conversation might have gone as follows:

"Dad, I need ten dollars for unexpected repairs on my bike."

"What happened to your bike?"

"I let Jimmy borrow it to get some things at the store for his mother and he ran over a nail. The innertube is torn and I've got to replace it. My allowance wasn't enough to pay for bicycle repairs."

"All right, son, here is the money."

Budgeting is based on current operations and future plans—with an avenue for appeal if new programs or unexpected expenses turn up. Like other activities, the library must have income. It cannot operate effectively for long without it. As a dynamic, evolving, ever-changing service, it must have funds from some source—even an allowance from the head of the household called the congregation.

"Just how much money does the library need?" Would you be prepared with an answer? In order to take advantage of

the opportunity to ask for funds when an opportunity presents itself, figure out how much you will need for the coming year and why. Begin with a plan and add up the cost.
Don't keep it to yourself. Tell those in positions of authority
what you need and what you hope to achieve.

Get into the Church's Budget

Income for the library should be an item in the church's
budget. Ask that the library be included.

Allocations. When we were still quite small, my sister and
I used to get an allowance once a week. Generally, we made
no plans about spending it until we received it. Then it was
gone within the day, spent usually on impulse for some tran-
sient interest. The amount we received was based on what
the family thought we ought to have rather than on our need.

Many congregational libraries operate this way too. They
receive an allowance—a dollar amount determined by the
sponsoring group—with no plan for spending it other than a
tacit understanding that it be used to buy resource materials
and supplies. At the time it is allocated, the librarian and/or
the book selection committee begins to buy books and other
materials, until the money is gone. It is not unusual to find
that funds have run out before the end of the year. It is
difficult, however, to obtain an amount above one's allowance unless a strong case can be made for a specific amount
to satisfy a specific one-time need. And when anticipated
income is unpredictable, it is hard to plan much beyond the
current year. Bright new projects often have to wait for the
next budget allocation, which may vary from year to year.

Line Item Budgets

A better system first identifies projected library needs. Then,
don't wait. Ask in advance for the amount you need to support the library's programs.

List major categories of expenses. Each category is a "line" in the library's budget. Here is a very simple listing: Resource materials, Equipment and supplies, Operating expenses. A slightly expanded list might contain additional categories, such as: Staff salaries, Resource materials, Supplies, Equipment rentals, Services (miscellaneous), Telephone and postage, Association memberships, and Continuing education.

Then be more specific. Break each category (line item) into its major parts, if any. Here is an example:

Preparing a Budget and Summary Sheet

Staff salaries
Part-time librarian.
Resource materials
Books (including pamphlets), subscriptions, audiovisual materials, and other nonprint items (games, etc.).
Supplies
Cataloging supplies, mending and repair, record-keeping (circulation, etc.), binding and storage, and promotion supplies.
Equipment
Audio cassette player.
Rentals
Filmstrips and videotapes.
Services-Miscellaneous
Maintenance, binding, and storytelling.
Telephone and postage
Association memberships
Church and Synagogue Library Association.
Continuing education
Correspondence courses, spring workshop, and CSLA annual conference.

Draw three columns beside each of these items. Label the columns last year's, this year's and next year's expenditures. The first two columns will be actual figures as near as they can be determined. The third will be estimated, based on the previous rate of spending. Example:

Category	Last year	This year	Next year
Resource materials			
Books	$	$	$
Subscriptions	$	$	$
Audiovisual materials	$	$	$
Other	$	$	$
Total Resources	$	$	$

Prepare a summary sheet of all the totals, as follows:

Category	Last year	This year	Next year
Staff salaries	$	$	$
Resource materials	$	$	$
Supplies	$	$	$
Equipment	$	$	$
Rentals	$	$	$
Services - Misc.	$	$	$
Telephone and postage	$	$	$
Association memberships	$	$	$
Continuing education	$	$	$
Total budget	$	$	$

If the estimated amount for next year is significantly different from previous years, explain it with a note. For example: "Ten percent has been added to allow for inflation."

A line item budget will tell you how much income you need to operate as you have in the past. If unusual expenditures are anticipated—perhaps for a new program—it is best to present this as a proposal for separate funding. In that way your regular operating budget will not be held up by a possibly controversial addition.

In a separate proposal, state the objective to be gained and the amount of money needed for it. In other words, describe what you want, the cost in dollars, and the benefits to be derived. For example, the library would like to purchase a new book truck. It costs approximately $300. The truck will be used to wheel a collection of books to the narthex each Sunday so they can circulate at that busy traffic intersection.

The truck will carry books related to the topic of the sermon that Sunday. It will reach more people and therefore make better use of the library's resources.

A well-documented request is businesslike. It proves you have thought it through carefully, have investigated what is available and the cost, and have a specific plan in mind that will further the goals of the library. In addition, try to anticipate other questions and be prepared with the answers. If space and traffic flow might appear to be a problem, draw up a floor plan to show (a) where the book truck will be located in the narthex on Sunday and (b) where it will be stored at other times when it is not in use. Such efficiency gains respect for your request, and that's the first step toward getting it approved.

Program Budgeting

Program budgeting is based entirely on goals and objectives rather than on operating expenses. Program budgeting is akin to writing a mini-proposal for every library activity you wish to have funded, within the context of long-range plans.

Begin planning with the objectives that support the library's goals. List them in priority order. Typical objectives are specific. Examples are: (1) provide a 4,000-volume collection of multimedia resources for the people and programs of the church by (date); (2) catalog all incoming materials and have them available for use within two weeks of receipt; (3) promote the library, its resources, and services according to the following schedule . . . ; (4) recruit and train three new members for the library staff by September (year); (5) establish an ongoing service for shut-ins . . . , etc.

In *With No Fear of Failure*, Keith Miller and Tom J. Fatjo, Jr. talk about creative dreaming, identifying goals and constructing action plans. Action planning, they say, is "taking a goal—any size—and breaking it down into the separate tasks or requirements which will lead to its accomplishment. Each task or requirement then becomes a smaller goal for which a specific action plan can be made."[1]

Begin constructing action plans by identifying the programs that will accomplish each objective and the specific projects within each one. One program is the multimedia resource collection (the first objective above). This could involve two projects: (a) needs assessment (to survey and identify the information resources needed) and (b) resource selection (to select, order and receive materials). Each project will have activities, which often break down into smaller work packages. A chart like that on page 14 makes it easy to see the elements of an action plan, including the deadlines (timetable) and estimated costs. Do this for each program. Then, to determine the overall cost, add up the costs of all the steps.

Strategic Planning

Strategic planning is having options available, such as levels of programming. When you ask for all the money you need to fully support your programs at their maximum effectiveness, with "all the frills," sometimes you will be surprised by receiving it. But full support cannot always be granted. If not, choices must be made.

Develop options. Plan your programs in three sizes: small, medium, and large. Small will be those basic programs that must be funded completely. An example might be the cataloging and preparing of required media materials for use in the church school. An expansion beyond this level makes the program medium, or large.

Identify any programs which might be stretched over more than one year. These might be the preparation of minisermons on cassette tapes for the shut-ins; instead of each month, an option is to prepare them for Christmas and Easter. Decide which programs are most important, and the steps within the programs that should be undertaken first—if you have the funds.

Assign priorities. With a three-level priority rating, number one would mean the program (or step) is absolutely essential this year; number two that it is essential, but could be defer-

ACTIVITY PLAN - 1984

Program: *Collection of Multimedia Resources (Ongoing $)*

Project: Needs Assessment (Recurs annually - $300)

Review of collection	Discussion with leaders & teachers	Consultation with pastor	Survey of congregation
	($50)		($250)
Jan. 15: Look over reference requests	*Attend planning meetings	*Obtain sermon topics	*Sep. 15:* Prepare & distribute questionnaire ($200)
Jan. 30: Review shelves & shelf list	*Feb. 14:* Hold a tea ($50)	**Send reviews for comment	*Sep. 30:* Evaluate results of survey
Feb. 10: Identify subject needs	Aug. 1: List needed resources		*Oct. 10:* Distribute results of evaluation ($50)

*As scheduled
**As received

red if necessary; number three that it is not really essential, but would help fulfill the objectives of the library.

The total cost of all number one priority items is the minimum budget acceptable to accomplish your basic objectives.

That figure plus the cost of all number two priority items is a budget you would like to have and one that would keep the library growing. All priority items added together would provide full funding for all your planned programs for the year.

After you have done your homework in this way, you are in a position to negotiate. You know the minimum amount acceptable, the amount it would be nice to have, and the amount that will completely support the entire program plan.

The budget cycle. Budget planning begins long before the actual church budget is adopted. Usually, a timetable is established that sets a date by which all requests for budget funds must be in to the Finance Committee. Sometimes these requests must channel through committees or groups, to be discussed and incorporated with other unit requests, before they are added to the overall proposed church budget.

Find out (1) when your library budget request is due and (2) to whom it should be given. Give the review groups adequate time to consider it. Be prompt in observing the deadlines for each. For example:

Action	Due date
Library budget to Education Committee	---
Education Committee budget to Finance Committee	---
Finance Committee budget to Administrative Board	---

When budget planning first begins, contact the other groups that sometimes allocate amounts of money to the library from their own budgets. Present to them a progress report about the library—its activities, successes, and future plans. Be enthusiastic. Help them to feel that they have contributed to your success. Communication like this will help to assure continuing support.

In summary. Strategic planning is based on one's purpose (goals), the broad objectives that support this purpose, and specific programs to achieve these objectives.

The statement of purpose tells why you are developing a library ministry. Try not to limit yourself to too narrow a view. This is the framework on which all else is built—the solid foundation as well as the guiding star.

Broad objectives tell how you propose to fulfill the purpose. It is a statement of the general plan for providing services and for whom.

Programs to carry out the objectives include selecting and ordering materials, cataloging and circulating them, promoting their use, etc. A timetable for completion and an estimate of the cost provides a businesslike basis for requesting financial support.

When levels of programming are identified, with a price tag for each, decisions and choices about the programs are easier for a manager to make. You begin to decide just how important each program (and each part of a program) really is.

3

SUPPLEMENTING YOUR INCOME

The sun shone through the stained-glass window and engulfed the elderly man sitting in the front pew. As the sun's warmth penetrated his clothing he straightened his shoulders and looked around to the source. A peaceful smile came over his face as he gazed at the beautiful window aglow in the sunlight.

A short while before, the congregation had given this stained-glass window as a gift to honor their long-time and much-loved former minister, who now was enjoying the sun's benediction. The gift was an appropriate tribute and lasting evidence of their mutual affection. Not so apparent, but a reinforcement of this tribute, were books about stained-glass windows that had been donated to the library. They were handsome volumes, amply illustrated with stained-glass windows, in color. The books would be used by readers who wished to know more about such windows, as well as by the church schoolteachers who needed good illustrations and background information for teaching. This also pleased the man in whose honor it was done. He had worked hard to set up a program of education and inspiration.

A gift is twice blessed. It benefits both the giver and the receiver. A gift for the library, however, is thrice blessed. It also benefits the people who use the library. These gifts provide books and other materials, as well as equipment, that otherwise might not be available. Therefore, gifts should be encouraged.

Having said that, I hasten to add that accepting gifts must be done with some care. Relics from someone's attic, topics

not suited for your library, or unsuitable furnishings should
be declined. This takes finesse and diplomacy, and a firmly
established library policy helps.

Accepting Gifts and Legacies

From the beginning, establish general guidelines regarding
the acceptance of gifts and legacies.

Selection policy. Review your book-selection policy. Dig
out your long-range plans for building the library—plans for
what will be offered, how and where. All gifts should con-
form to these policies and plans.

A policy for accepting gifts will help you determine if the
books from Dr. Jones' library are of value to your church or
synagogue library and whether or not to accept Mrs. Brown's
offer of an easy chair, lamp, or hand-crafted bookcase. The
established policy protects you from having to accept a gift
that you really do not want or need. At the same time, it is
a reasonable and acceptable explanation to the would-be
donor for your saying "No thanks."

Flexibility. The administration of this policy need not make
you inflexible in regard to serving your congregation. For
example, you might want to accept a gift on occasion that you
really do not plan to make a part of the library—as a convenience for the giver. A parishioner is moving from the area and
wishes to dispose of two boxes of books; some of them are
children's books; some might be of value to the library but
not all. Many libraries take whatever is offered so they can
screen out any usable items to keep. Let the donor know that
you plan to do this. Tell him or her that you will keep the
books that the library can use (that fit your selection policy)
and will pass along the others to another library or put them
in the next used-book sale sponsored by the youth group.
Generally, donors will be happy to know that their offerings
will be put to some good use.

Know What You Want

"Our circle would like to give a gift to the library," a parishioner half-whispered to the librarian at a Sunday morning coffee hour and, leaning closer, confided, "in honor of our circle chairman."

"How nice," the librarian responded warmly, "that will please both of us."

"Do you have anything really nice to suggest? Anything the library would particularly like to have, that would be suitable?" the parishioner added.

"We have a whole list of good books that we would like to have," the librarian responded with enthusiasm. "Come into the library after the service and we will pick out an appropriate title—within the price range you had in mind." Her confidante nodded assent just as others joined them at the social hour.

The "want" file. Develop a "want" file, a list of titles and equipment the library needs, based on long-range plans and a careful review of the collection of materials you already have. Separate the file into price ranges. For example, items that cost less than $10, from $10 to $50, over $50. Then, when a potential donor asks what the library would like to have, you are ready to answer—specifically.

Some people like to choose gift books that relate to a particular interest they have, such as social concerns, church history, or missionary work. For this reason, it is wise to have as well-rounded a list as possible. Scan the booklists and reviews of books in newspapers and periodicals. Browse through the displays at your local religious bookstore. Carry a 3" x 5" pad of paper with you. When you come upon books that would be useful additions to your collection, write down the title, author, publisher, date of publication and price—one title to a sheet. Later, check to see if you already have it in the collection or if a copy is on order. Keep an eye out for good reference books, as these generally are more expensive and are welcome additions as gifts. Keep the congregation informed of library needs; this encourages the giving of gifts.

Memorials

Memorial gifts are important sources of funds. Betty McMichael reported that 10 percent of the 400 congregational libraries to which she sent a questionnaire responded that memorials were their primary source of funding.[1]

The librarian of Cuyahoga County Public Library, Garfield Heights, Ohio, speaks highly of asking for memorials. She says, "The deceased will be remembered whenever someone uses the book or reads the book. Eventually the book will be discarded, but not as quickly as the flowers, and more people will see and enjoy the remembrance."[2]

"Most of the additions to the collection in recent years have been through memorials," reports the minister of a church in Santa Fe, New Mexico. "Each new volume is suitably inscribed and the names of people memorialized also are included in a large display case in the Tower Room of Holy Faith Church. This is a library annex complete with several book and tract racks."[3]

A dentist and ardent booklover, Dr. Charles King, left an endowment of $15,000 for the construction of a library and rectory for the small, twenty-year-old congregation that existed in Andalusia, in the rural area north of Philadelphia. For many years the Church of the Redeemer flourished and its library was the center of activity both for the church and the community school.[4]

The Norman Hjorth Memorial Library of Trinity United Presbyterian Church in Cherry Hill, New Jersey, was dedicated as a memorial to the husband of Charlotte Hjorth, church librarian for fourteen years. Norman worked closely with his wife in founding and maintaining the library. Friends contributed gifts enabling the church to acquire new bookshelves, a card catalog, reading tables, and a check-out desk.[5]

An unusual memorial gift was given by Mrs. Forrest Carpenter, librarian of the Oak Grove Lutheran Church in Richfield, New Mexico. As a memorial to her mother, she purchased, processed, and catalogued enough books to set up a small beginning library at another church—Our Savior's Lutheran Church in Stanley.[6]

Appreciation

Memorials are expressions of love. The library provides an avenue for such declarations of affection and regard. These expressions should be openly appreciated.

In addition to placing bookplates in gift books, plaques on memorial equipment, and names on entire libraries, there are other very practical ways of showing appreciation for gifts. Write letters of thanks to the donors, to persons honored, and to the families of persons memorialized. A little "thank you" note can mean a lot.

The Memorial Corner Provides A Setting for A Story Hour

Dollar-Stretching Ideas

Try to get the most for your money. Look for ways that will help you spend your gift funds and budgeted money wisely.

Shop for bargains. Watch for sales of new books. Sometimes these are announced in the newspaper, other times they will be advertised by a flyer sent to the home. Look for the "bargain table" sometimes featured in retail bookstores with new books offered at marked-down prices. Go browsing with your list of needed topics and titles.

Discount bookstores offer current new books at reduced prices all year long. These are found in most large cities. Look in the yellow pages of the telephone book under "Book dealers - Retail."

Wherever you buy books, inquire about standard library discounts. Compare the discounts given by retail stores, wholesale dealers, and other services (such as denominational publishing houses) that supply books by mail. (See chapter 6 on Ordering Materials.)

Buy paperback editions. Many excellent books come in paperback editions. These are cheaper than the hardcover editions, so you will be able to purchase more books for the same amount of money. Books with a short "shelf-life," such as current controversial topics or study books, should be purchased in paperback anyway. Usually these books have high interest for a concentrated period of time and then are seldom read again. Paperback books have other benefits. They are lightweight and easy to carry around. Young people, especially, like them. Set up a special display of the paperback books to capitalize on their special appeal.

Trade and buy used books. If you have two copies of a good book (and need only one), it would be nice to be able to trade one copy for something else. Where? How? There are both formal and informal channels.

Contact other local librarians with similar subject interests. Give each other first choice of books you do not need. Have a new and used book exchange with the congregation or with your group of librarians. Call it a "Flea Market," a "Swap Shop" or "Ten Cents a Choice," but plan an informal swap table. Advertise it in advance so people will come prepared to trade. This has been done successfully at conferences and workshops such as those sponsored by the Lutheran Church Library Association, the Church Library Council (Greater Washington, D.C., area), and the Church and Synagogue Library Association.

The proprietor of a used bookstore in California says, "Trading and buying used books instead of new books are two excellent ways to stretch the available money." She adds that you can trade books with other libraries or you can trade with a used-book dealer for dollar credit.[7]

Outside Support

"I have a dream," says Betty McMichael of Boulder, Colorado, "that some day a philanthropic individual or agency will plant thriving church libraries across the country, in the style of an Andrew Carnegie or perhaps a Johnny Appleseed."[8]

It might not be in the style of Andrew Carnegie, but grant money, donations, and free materials are available from outside the congregation.

Grants. Approach the major businesses in your neighborhood and ask for a donation toward building your library. Offer to advertise their generosity through an article in the church paper or a plaque hung on the wall. This would be good public relations for a local business.

If your library plans to serve the entire community because there is no public library nearby, it would be quite appropriate for you to ask the administrators of local government to help support this service. Don't apologize for expecting financial support and be prepared to tell them how this will benefit the community. For example, if the church library provides a place to meet and the background materials for a home-computer hobby group, this activity will help to keep the youth of the community occupied with productive (nondestructive) pursuits. This, in some communities, could help to solve a problem. It also could help to support the library and be an outreach activity for the congregation.

Free materials. The only purpose of the American Bible Society is "the distribution of the Holy Scriptures without doctrinal note or comment and without profit." They will donate bibles to needy individuals or churches. Write, explaining the need, to ABS, 1865 Broadway, New York, NY 10023.

Sometimes publishers or retail book dealers will donate free books to libraries that are just beginning. Look over the collection of religious books at your local public library, at another congregation's library, or a seminary library. Jot down the name of the publishers of books you particularly admire. Ask the librarian to help you find their addresses, or inquire at the local bookstore. Publishers' addresses can be found in the annual *Books in Print* (R. R. Bowker Co., 1180 Avenue of the Americas, New York, NY 10036).

Free and inexpensive pamphlets are available from a variety of sources. A regular column entitled "Potpourri" in *Church & Synagogue Libraries* (Bryn Mawr, PA, Church and Synagogue Library Association, bimonthly) lists such materials. Another source is a special page titled "Checklist" in both the monthly *Library Journal* and the *School Library Journal* (R. R. Bowker Co.).

Borrowing money. Mary Oeler, director of religious education at St. Ignatius parish in Whitfield, Pennsylvania, reports she has had experiences in two libraries with borrowing the funds needed. Most recently she borrowed $100 from the pastor of their parish. She says she has no fears about repaying the debt because in a previous parish, St. Joseph's in Duquesne, Pennsylvania, they began their library by borrowing $1,000 for shelves, furniture, and books. The loan was repaid in less than a year. To do this, they made jars to look like banks and marked them "Thank You" on the outside. These were placed at each of the five church doors every Sunday, with an explanation of how the money was being used. Each week they collected $20 to $50 in odd change which church members put into the jars.[9]

Formal borrowing of funds, from a bank for example, should be done only through your chain of command. Get the approval of the church managers. More than likely, if borrowing is approved, it will be done and papers signed by the individual(s) in the church who have been empowered to enter into such contracts.

Fund-Raising Events

Fund-raising events should never be held just to make money. They should have some other purpose as well, such as to educate, to inspire, or to amuse. These events should be tasteful and in keeping with the library's image.

"People like to get something for their money, even when the money is going to a good cause. That's why fund-raising events are often more successful than outright solicitations for contributions," according to an article in *Changing Times*. The writer offers the following advice: "To succeed, the event must be well planned. Select a reliable and energetic member of the group to head the whole project, get as many members of the sponsoring organization as possible to participate, have a specific dollar target, and try to come up with something original and appealing to your potential patrons."[10]

A freelance advertising and public relations executive offers ideas for a mythical cake sale, a silent auction, home tours, stationery sale, handcraft and boutique items, and a Safari excursion.[11] Another writer suggests bazaars, show-houses, parties, and auctions.[12]

Additional ideas for fund-raising activities are described in *Getting the Books Off the Shelves; Making the Most of Your Congregation's Library* (New York, NY: Hawthorn Books, 1975) and *Promotion Planning* (Bryn Mawr, PA: Church and Synagogue Library Association, 1975).

Before you begin, however, it is best to check with the administration of your church or synagogue to determine general policy in regard to fund-raising endeavors. Some congregations do not believe in raising money in this way. If so, you will need to look for other avenues of supplementary support, such as gifts, special church offerings for the library, or fines for overdue books. (For the latter, see chapter 7, Keeping Track of Resources.)

4

LOCATING FOR GREATEST USE

"Professor Defends Live-in Chicken Coop."

This eye-catching headline introduced a story about a thirty-five-year-old doctoral candidate and professor of economics who had converted a 9' x 12' chicken coop into a place to live. He had patched it with discarded materials and equipped it with a refrigerator, telephone, desk lamp, hot plate, toaster oven, desk, stuffed chair, folding chairs, dresser, raised wooden bed, cabinet, hatchet, and shotgun. The location, however, was in someone's backyard and the county's Health Board declared his habitation too small and too primitive for human habitation.[1]

So, before you find yourself a closet and start fixing it up for a library, find out if the authorities of your organization approve of the location and the intended use. Find out what suitable space is available. If you must settle for that closet, know the kind of place you really need for the library and keep working toward it.

Find the Right Place

The library is a service-oriented center—a ministry—and ministry means dealing with people. Therefore, the library should be located near the people it hopes to serve. Ideally, it should be easy to find and easy to enter. The location is certain to influence how well it is able to fulfill its purpose.

Purpose. Consider again your basic goals. What are you going to use the location for and how? A collection of books only, for adults only, will not need the same location (or size room) as a multimedia learning center for children. Here is an example of how the purpose of a library influenced its setting:

The Washington Hebrew Congregation in Washington, D.C., has an adult library for the congregation. (It also has a children's library in a separate location, a part of the religious school.) Their librarian describes it as follows: "The Temple Library enjoys an excellent location within the building. As one enters the synagogue the library-lounge is directly across the central lobby. Double doors open into the walnut-paneled room and face a window wall which opens onto a grassy terrace extending to a wooded park area beyond the synagogue grounds. At all seasons of the year this picture wall provides a view of quiet, natural beauty, bringing a sense of peace and communion with God."[2]

Not all libraries begin with a location that is quite so ideal. Some change their goals and purposes as the years go by and this alters their need for location and space.

St. Lucia Library at Our Lady Queen of Martyrs Church in Birmingham, Michigan, began in a limited church vestibule space and now is flourishing in a room designed for the library in the new church edifice built in 1965.[3]

The Dominick Memorial Library at Gethsemane Lutheran Church in Hopkins, Minnesota, had a bookshelf with glass doors as its first location. Later it moved to a room of its own in the basement of the education building. Finally, it moved to a main-floor location in the church school wing of the main building. This location is beside the main stream of traffic between the sanctuary and the church school classrooms and across the hall from the church lounge. Their librarian reports, "Here easier access for both adults and children, plus much-needed shelf space will give the library more opportunities for service to the whole congregation."[4]

At St. Peter's Episcopal Church in Lakewood, Ohio, the purposes of the library changed. When his small son came home with a black box slung over his shoulder containing a filmstrip viewer, filmstrip, and script and all excited about the new Learning Center at school, the Rev. Richard M. Morris was motivated to find out more about the Center. His talks with the instructors and his observation of the youngsters' fascination with their projects were a contrast with the church school classes still gathered around a rectangular table. He was stimulated to do something for the church in the way of a parish learning center. He tells this story:

> Next door to the old-office-turned-Library and Learning Center was another small office . . . a perfect place for reference books, a round table (36 inches in diameter), and five chairs. With the installation of a filmstrip projector with a wide-angle lens, a record player (or a tape recorder) with a seven-plug jack, and earphones, this room became one of the group listening areas. We created another small area for study and group listening in the main room of the Learning Center. Finally, we built five study 'carrels,' in which we made provision for rear-screen filmstrip viewers, tape recorders, slide projectors, record players, and earphones.[5]

Accessibility. The library, no matter what it's called, should be easy for potential patrons to find.

Writes Marian S. Johnson:

> If a library is to be used by the entire membership, it should be near the center of traffic, near an outside entrance to the church school, and on the ground floor. Alternatives when the space of a separate room is not available would include (1) one end of the social hall, (2) a corner of the hallway of the education building, (3) a classroom corner, (4) a mobile bookcase rolled in the way of would-be readers, (5) a large closet off the narthex—"book nook," or, (6) part of a lounge room.[6]

Identification. Let the members of the congregation know where you are. Hang signs and tack up posters. Place an attractive and legible sign outside the door that says **library.** Post the library's room number on all bulletin boards. Remind people in announcements from the pulpit and in publications that are handed out or sent to the homes.

Wolf Von Eckardt writes:

> To find the lion house in Washington's National Zoo, just follow the paw prints on the paved walkway. To find the Museum of Natural History on the Mall, just look at one of the three-dimensional orientation maps beside the roadways. It will show you not only where the building is located but what it looks like. The lion tracks and the maps of the Mall are parts of recently installed graphic information systems that make it easy to find your way.[7]

Try drawing a graphic map of the church floor plan and have a red arrow point to the library. Post this at main locations.

Room Environment

Is your library room itself "inviting"? It should be easy to enter, a light and airy room with adequate space, and practically yet attractively furnished.

Easy to enter. An open door is inviting. Take a look at your entrance. When the door is open, does it tend to block access to a part of the library, such as the children's corner or the periodical shelving? If so, investigate the possibilities of either moving the shelving or changing the door so it swings out instead of in. All parts of the library should be open to view or, at least, be arranged so readers or browsers are led to their areas of interest. Easy accessibility promotes use.

Adequate space. The room should be large enough to provide the services you hope to offer and to allow for the possibility of expansion as the library and its services grow.

Review the programs you have planned. (See chapter 2 on Budgeting for Growth.) For the current levels of programming, list resources, equipment, and services required —preferably in the order of their importance. The room should provide adequately for those listed first, even if those listed last must be crowded—or be offered from another location— until better arrangements can be made.

Services	Resources	Materials/Equipment
Browsing	Books	Processing materials
Circulation	Periodicals	Shelving
Reference	Pictures	Book ends
Cataloging	Pamphlets/Clippings	Picture file
Viewing/Listening	Maps	Pamphlet boxes
Reading lists	Filmstrips	Table
Service to shut-ins	Records	Chairs
Visits from classes	Audio cassettes	Charging desk
Displays	College catalogs	Card catalog
Reviews	Models	Vertical file
Storytelling	Games/Kits	A-V files
		Viewers/Projectors
		Screens
		Storage closet

Add to this list the services, resources, and equipment needed to achieve your long-range plans—which might include a multimedia learning and information center, eventually tied into closed-circuit television.

Lighting and ventilation. A light and airy room is comfortable—for the individuals using the library and for the materials stored there.

A room needs good air circulation and as much daylight as possible. Try to avoid high humidity or dry heat. The first encourages the growth of mildew (especially on cloth or leather bindings) and the second tends to make paper or film become brittle and crack. The ideal library temperature is 70°. Materials do best when stored away from direct heat and relatively free of dust.

The Richfield Lutheran Church Library in Minneapolis is

an air-conditioned room. It features about 2,000 books, has a specially designed case for maps and pictures of Bible times, and includes a collection of records and a beginning cassette collection. Large display windows with glass shelving are located on either side of the door leading into the hall and are directly across the room from another door leading into a delightful courtyard complete with a fountain.[8]

Most libraries have overhead lights, but sometimes these are not enough. Study your room. Do you need additional light? At the librarian's desk or by the lounge chair? Consider the possibilities. Indirect lighting, a desk lamp or a table lamp with a good field of light might create interesting effects and add to the attractiveness of the room as well as the visibility. Visit your local lamp shop for ideas.

Floors, Walls, and Windows

The room itself needs a basic color scheme. Begin with attractive curtains and build a color scheme around them. Use light colors for small rooms, such as pale green or beige. Although you may have vinyl asbestos tile on the floor, carpet the library—eventually.

Carpeting was provided long after the Bethesda United Methodist Church Library was in existence. It was presented as a gift from the Katering Kates, a group within the women's society. It softens the library's concrete block walls (which are painted a light cream) and adds warmth to the room. Floor-to-ceiling draw draperies open and close over two windows and cover the expanse of the one wall. Colors from the draperies are picked up in the carpet, lounge chairs, and directional signs.

Attractive decor. Enlist the aid of the people who use the library to help make it more attractive. Kenneth H. Sayers, a young adult/community service librarian with the Salinas, Kansas, Public Library did this with surprising results. He canvassed the local high school and the teachers and enlisted a corps of teenagers to tackle the job of creating a young adult section in the library. The result was successful:

One wall of the 1,200 sq. ft. area became a colorful mural. Carpeting was created from rug samples, cut and glued into a crazy-quilt pattern . . . . Large bean-bag chairs were made from free patterns and sale-price denim. They hung houseplants from the beamed ceilings and made spool-top tables supported by pipes.[9]

Libraries traditionally provide a quiet setting, but newer facilities have pleasing and comfortable surroundings as well. The one in Long Branch in Montgomery County, Maryland, has a modern high-ceilinged building that is light and airy and furnished with colorful, comfortable chairs.[10]

Remember the general character of your own congregation—the people who use your library. Decorate and make the library attractive to them, so they will feel comfortable enough to be at home there.

Floor Plans

Draw up a floor plan to help make the best use of available space. If you are fortunate enough to have an architect in your congregation, get him or her to help. Draw the overall plan and identify the basic areas of activity.

Overall plan. Begin with a sheet of graph paper. Establish a scale, such as one square on the paper equals one square foot of room space. Measure the room, the windows and doors. Draw this on the graph paper, to scale, recording the number of linear feet represented by each line. Study the space with which you have to work, considering the limitations imposed by the location of the doors and windows.

The Sebring Memorial Library in the Chevy Chase, Maryland, Baptist Church, has a large picture window that looks out into the hallway. On either side of the window are two built-in glass-front exhibit cases where books and other objects can be displayed. Yet the room itself is large enough for all three age groups to each have a table (all three were donated as memorials). The audiovisual collection is housed in a separate room connected with the library.

Arrangement. Consider your main areas of activity, such as entry room, shelving for the general collection and the children's collection, tables for reading or study, card catalog, workroom and storage, etc. Is your service for adults only or do you hope to provide multimedia materials for all ages? Will you have viewing and listening stations? Do you plan a collection of art such as framed reproductions of master-pieces? Will there be room for small classes to use the mul-timedia resources and equipment? These things must all be considered.

Sometimes less than ideal space must be used to best ad-vantage. Jim Clark, once a workshop leader with Remington Rand on library room-and-equipment, suggests on pages 34–35 plans for (a) a small, unsuitable room made usable and (b) an ideal kind of room for basic library services.

For your own plan, try cutting out furnishings to scale, so you can "play" with the arrangement before it is drawn onto the plan. Obtain a library supply catalog to get average mea-surements for standard library furniture, such as shelving, card catalog, etc.

Electrical outlets. Be sure to include in your plan such items as electrical outlets. When our new education building was designed, we were concerned only that electrical outlets were installed in the walls rather than in the floors. Then, after the shelving was in and the books in place, we discov-ered that most of the outlets were hidden behind the shelv-ing. This did not make them unusable, since the shelving had open backs, but it did make the outlets more difficult to locate.

Equipment

Brother David Martin of Portland, Oregon, emphasizes the importance of selecting library furnishings: "Although the trained librarian welcomes a once-in-a-lifetime chance of participation in the planning of a new library, he realizes the responsibility involved in an undertaking which affords no opportunity to acquire skill through trial and error."[11]

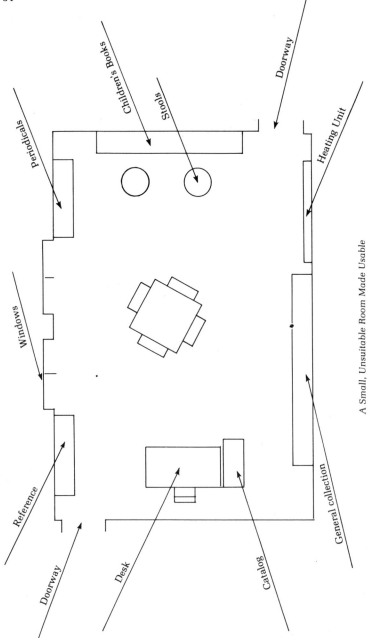

Children's Books

Stools

Doorway

Periodicals

Heating Unit

Windows

A Small, Unsuitable Room Made Usable

Reference

General collection

Doorway

Desk

Catalog

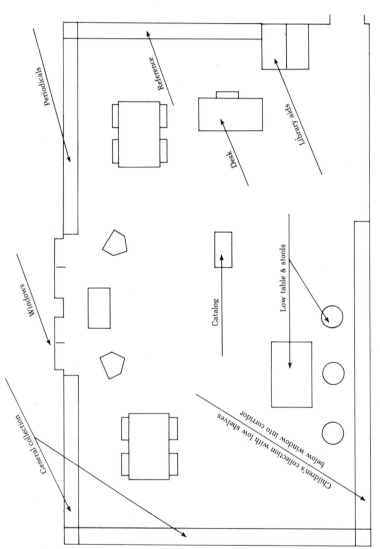

Periodicals

Reference

Library aids

Desk

Windows

Catalog

Low table & stools

General collection

Children's collection with low shelves
below window into corridor

A Room Suitable for Basic Library Services

When you plan a library and select library furniture, you have to be right the first time. So it is wise to prepare yourself for this responsibility by reading current articles on the subject, visiting other libraries (and school media centers), and talking with those who have had experience (other librarians and furniture dealers).

Identify basic needs. Look at the floor plan again and its areas of activity. What do you need to acquire as furnishings? Review the list of materials and equipment you compiled when first considering the room and location (see previous section on "adequate space"). Is it still in order of importance? If not, arrange it that way.

Basic furnishings might include: shelving (books/magazines-adults/children), table and chairs (reading/study), desk and chair (librarian/charging), card catalog, picture file (teaching pictures), and vertical file (maps/pamphlets).

Basic auxiliary equipment might include: book ends, charging tray, typewriter, pamphlet boxes, A-V storage files, A-V projectors, and screen.

Mark the items that will be your first purchase. This is your shopping list.

Consider suitability. Furniture and equipment comes in a variety of sizes, finishes, colors, and shapes—as well as prices. So before you start shopping, think of the desired qualities that will make a difference in your selection. For example, what type furniture will best fit the room and the purposes of the library? Will you want to move it later to larger quarters? Consider the pros and cons of built-ins vs. standard library furniture, modern or traditional, wood or metal, as well as size, color, and finish. Consider the cost. Cost alone, however, should not be the only deciding factor.

Suitable furniture is practical, establishes the decor of the room, and fits comfortably into the space. The size is in proportion to the area allocated (not crowded), to scale (comfortable for the readers to use), and adequate for the collection (enough capacity for housing and using). As an example, you would choose a small charging desk for a small room and child-size chairs for the children's corner.

Flexible furniture is practical because it can be relocated when the library grows or new services require a reallocation of space. Although built-in shelving is functional, it does not have this advantage. The shelving, either wood or metal, that is purchased from standard library supply sources can be purchased a unit at a time. If you spread out your acquisitions over a period of years, you also spread out the cost.

Quality furniture is practical because it lasts longer. It is constructed of solid wood—usually hard maple, oak, or birch—constructed with water-resistant glue (glued under heat and pressure), with reinforcing blocks at stress points. Machine bolts connect bases and cornice tops as well as leg assemblies. The wear-resistant finish is achieved by application of stain, sealer, and an overcoat baked to superhardness. Some table tops are finished with a 1/16" high-pressure plastic laminate face sheet for added protection. Finishes are custom matched at no extra charge, which is especially important when the units are not purchased all at the same time.

Four imaginative designs for shelving that might be used in a congregational library are described in an article in *Church & Synagogue Libraries*.[12] These were taken from a booklet called *Design for Paperbacks* (Educational Facilities Laboratories, Inc., 477 Madison Avenue, New York, NY 10022), the result of a conference regarding educational facilities for schools and colleges.

Compare suppliers. Just as there are many manufacturers who make cars, there are many dealers who supply standard library furniture. However, the major suppliers generally have catalogs which often can be obtained free of charge. (See the list of Library Suppliers in the Appendix.) Some of the denominational publishing houses, through their general supply catalogs, also offer items such as audiovisual equipment, storage cabinets and screens, as well as charging trays, book supports, and shelf label holders; some even carry small-size card catalogs.

Select and Order

Choose the items you need to order, considering size, style, cost, and quantity. Basic furniture has some standard characteristics, which are described in detail in the library supply catalogs.

Shelving: All standard shelving is 3-feet wide. Standard depths of shelves are 8″ for average books, 10″ for reference books, and 12″ for children's books or for periodical units with sloping shelves.

Joyce Holbrook, librarian of Good Samaritan United Methodist Church in Edina, New Mexico, offers the following suggestion:

> Experiencing a discouraging problem of books falling down or over every time another book was removed, a solution was discovered ... colorful, plastic vegetable bins were purchased at a discount store and they were placed on the shelves in alternating colors. Each bin has approximately six to ten books in it and when the children come in, they can take a bin on the floor with them and have their own little private book selection area.[13]

Open shelves invite browsing. Generally, they are placed against the walls, but not in front of windows, doors or heating elements. The Fourth Presbyterian Church in Bethesda placed aisle-type shelving units on either side of high windows. They extend out into the room and create semiprivate study areas large enough for a table and chairs.

If space is a real problem, consider mobile shelves. Two shelving units can be placed face to face, with back panels facing out. Hinge the units together on one side to swing open. Place a lock on the other side, so the units can be closed and locked when not in use. Mount casters on the bottom. The units will move easily from place to place, even to storage when not in use.

If cost dictates that you must build your own shelving,

follow the plans and specifications found in the supply catalogs. Copy the real thing.

Periodical rack: Adjustable sloping shelves are available that fit into the regular shelving units. These shelves provide a ledge for current magazines to be displayed face out. A straight shelf below each sloping shelf holds back issues of the displayed magazine.

Separate, free-standing periodical racks are available also. These can be located anywhere in the room or against the wall. A "small" rack will hold up to twenty-two magazines.

Charging desk: This can be a desk for the librarian or a series of units assembled into an L- or U-shaped arrangement, with counter space, drawers for records and circulation supplies, and a place for files, desk, and typewriter. These assembled units are available in standing or sitting heights.

Let the size of your room determine the size charging desk you need. A 425-square-foot room would not need a charging desk larger than a desk. Desks are available with a right-hand drawer that is deep enough to hold the circulation file. Some models accommodate a typewriter within a compartment on one side.

Tables and chairs. Choose reading tables and chairs, as well as easy chairs for more relaxed reading, to fit the users and the decor of the room. Make sure they are suitable for the age group and the intended use.

Card catalog. The trays (drawers) for a card catalog are standard in size, to fit a 3" x 5" card. Each tray is equipped with a metal rod to hold the cards in file in case the tray is dropped. Each tray also has a label holder on the front of the drawer. Since the card catalog is an important investment, take care to purchase one large enough to allow for growth. What is the maximum size your library is expected to be? Estimate five catalog cards per book and 1,000 cards per drawer. A sectional card catalog allows flexibility for the expanding library since it can be purchased a section at a time as your library grows.

Once you have selected what you want, ask the supplier

to provide an estimate of the cost and the delivery date. Give him as much detail as possible. This will enable him to double check the measurements—just in case you miscalculated the size of the furniture as it was listed in the catalog. For example, shelving comes with end panels which add two inches to the length of a continuous tier.

Innovations

Imaginative extras can add life and fun to any library. For example, the librarian of Grace United Presbyterian Church in Council Bluffs, Iowa, reports: "Due to a lack of space, we had difficulty displaying magazines until we fastened a narrow board to the wall in a vertical position. Current magazines are ringed and hung on this board by using cup hooks. These can be readily seen when entering the library."[14]

Members of Wayne Presbyterian Church, Wayne, Pennsylvania, purchased three 6' strips of wood molding and sawed them into 3' strips—the exact width of the shelves. These they attached to the shelves, about two inches from the front, using two small thin nails for each strip. Then, to form a sloping shelf for magazines, they purchased bright yellow, heavy cardboard, cut it with a paper cutter to the proper size, and inserted it behind the molding. To form rests for the back top of the cardboard, extra adaptable shelf holders were inserted into the back row of holes, one on each side, about nine inches up from the shelf. The strip of molding keeps the magazines from sliding off the shelf and the heavy cardboard holds them at the proper angle to be seen.[15]

A unique way to brighten up furniture is reported by Jane Gardner, Youth Services Coordinator of the Yakima Valley, Washington, Regional Library. They launched a "Once in a Lifetime Great Cushion Contest" and involved their patrons. Based on characters in children's books, the children were asked to submit designs—on 20" x 20" paper using the colors in a standard pack of eight crayons. By using one design on each side of a pillow, they made ten pillows from the winning designs, which were submitted by children ranging in age from three to twelve. To transfer the designs, they traced them with fabric crayons. The tracings were placed face down on denimlike beige fabric and pressed with a hot iron. Then the fabric was sewn onto a cushion. "The cushions are bright and a real expression of children's creativity—just the right touch we needed for the area. All the children are enjoying them. . . . They are proud of their contribution to the library."[16]

Lorraine Pike of Milwaukee reports that on a bus tour taken by a group of church librarians, they discovered at the second stop, "an excellent example of imaginative and efficient use of a small library at the Holy Trinity Lutheran Church of West Allis. What fun it was to step up to the children's section between two tall, yellow, wooden giraffes."[17]

A library for preschool children was created out of a small room conveniently located next to the church library at the Abington, Pennsylvania, Presbyterian Church.

> Books for the preschool child were removed from the main library room. Colorful children's chairs were placed around a butterfly-shaped table. Bright green draperies with red lions sporting a white daisy on their tails, and reading books through their black-rimmed spectacles, were added to the growing decor. A hooked rug, and finally, a table-desk and chair for the librarian resulted in a cheerful room of learning for the preschool child. . . . The records are kept in an open "browser" unit built and donated by a member of the congregation.[18]

Take a look at your own library. How can you brighten it up or improve its serviceability? Try to make it a fun place to visit for reading, viewing, or listening—or even for working puzzles, making transparencies, or recording cassettes for a Bible class quiz. When the creative urge begins to stir, your library can become a showcase, too.

5

STAFFING AND SCHEDULING

It was a beautiful spring day. I sat with my morning coffee looking out the dining-room to the azaleas and dogwood trees in glorious bloom across the way. Across my line of sight a tree branch began to sway with some vigor. I looked for the cause, expecting to find a squirrel jumping from one branch to another. Instead, I was surprised to see a small sparrow bobbing at the end of the branch. How could such a small creature create so much effect? That made me realize with renewed appreciation that even a little bird can make a difference. Small talents can be used to create big results.

That's how it is in the library, too. Some church libraries flourish while others seem to need continuous rescue from languish and neglect. The difference usually is an individual who is willing to go out on a limb, someone who is willing to go to work enthusiastically, someone who really believes in the ministry of books and is able to relate to the needs of people, and someone with enough intelligence and imagination to be able to learn and teach others the basic skills of library organization, operation and outreach.

Choosing a Librarian

The librarian is a key person, setting the tone of the library, attracting and training staff helpers, and responding to the needs of individuals through a ministry of information. The selection of a librarian can be the most important decision that is made. It usually is the difference between a successful library or media center and one that just limps along.

Qualities. What makes a good librarian? Librarian Wes Daniels says, "The most important qualities are common sense, curiosity, concern for other people and intelligence—none of which can be taught. The rest consists mainly of mechanics, which are best learned by doing."[1]

Mary Eble of Fairview, Ohio, High School suggests, "If I were to pinpoint the most necessary qualification for the library media-specialist beginning a career, it would be enthusiasm." You can't be enthusiastic about something you don't like, something you don't believe in, or something second rate.[2]

"God is not so much interested in your ability as your availability," is the opinion of Louise Walker, librarian of the First Presbyterian Church in St. Petersburg, Florida. She responded to the challenge of being a church librarian, took some courses in library science as a senior citizen, and proceeded to reorganize the library. It's work she obviously loves—as evidenced by the touch of pride in her voice when she leads a tour through the library and the way she handles certain books as she pulls them off the shelf. She spends thirty or more hours a week at the library, greeting people with a bright smile and directing them to helpful resources. She spends other time building and caring for the collection, which almost doubled within five years after she took on the job. She also finds time to write a weekly column for the church bulletin. "I love my work in the library," she says.[3] Perhaps that is the ultimate qualification.

The volunteer librarian. How do you attract such a person to serve as church librarian? In most congregational libraries, the librarian is a volunteer worker who contributes time and talent without expectation of financial reward. The rewards are in a job well done and in the satisfaction of helping other people.

A volunteer is motivated by the desire to serve. Yet not all who might volunteer to be librarian will be acceptable. In addition to a desire to serve, they need to possess some degree of organizational ability and a willingness to learn standard library techniques, as well as an ability to work well with others—that crew of volunteer helpers as well as unpredictable patrons.

There are people who prefer to do things in their own way and alone. In a small library one person can do all the work and provide adequate library service to a limited community of users. As the library grows, however, teamwork and a sharing of the planning and the work become much more important. The librarian of a growing library media center will need to have a talent for leadership and a firm foundation in library policies and procedures in order to teach others, delegate work, and deal effectively with situations which require sensitivity, tact, and diplomacy.

Evaluate each volunteer. Does he or she really have what it takes to be a good librarian? (Perhaps another avenue of service would be more suitable?) A good volunteer librarian is a jewel to be treasured. Since no contract or other legal requirement holds a volunteer, use praise and encouragement, as often as necessary, to let your librarian know your appreciation.

The salaried employee. Some congregations pay their librarian for part-time work; the amount varies from a token fee to the standard hourly rate for professional librarians. A few larger congregations hire a librarian as a full-time member of the staff, along with the minister or the rabbi, the choir director or the cantor, and the paid custodians. This helps to ensure stability and continuity.

The Treasurer and the main office generally take care of salary payments—including necessary records, deductions, and arrangements for insurance, retirement, withholding taxes, etc. If the amount paid to an employee totals $50 or more during any one quarter of the year, they will file with the Internal Revenue Service an employer's quarterly tax return. Whatever the amount paid, they will provide the employee a completed "Wage and Tax Statement" (Form W-2). This is a record of the total amount paid during the year as wages or other compensation and the amounts deducted for Federal and other taxes.

Performance evaluations. The person to whom the librarian reports should conduct a year-end performance review, pointing out the strengths and the weaknesses in the librarian's performance. This is especially important if the librarian is paid and reappointed, or not, each year. It helps justify whichever action is taken. If the evaluation is especially good, it will help the administrative board decide if an increase in salary can be recommended.

The simplest performance evaluation is a conversation with the librarian about how things are going, followed by an informal report to the committee that handles staff relations. This might be sufficient. If a more formal report is required, an evaluation is written out, discussed with the librarian, and then presented to the committee with a summary of the discussion. To assist in the evaluation process, the smart librarian—volunteer or salaried—will prepare an annual report of library activities and accomplishments in advance of the review.

Recruiting Staff

The librarian is expected to recruit and train a staff of helpers, as needed. Generally, the staff will be made up of volunteer workers.

Requirements. There are many different tasks to be done and these require a variety of talents. Writing in School Library Journal, Elfrieda McCauley says:

> Volunteers tend circulation desks and perform technical processing tasks in the media centers. They create bulletin boards, letter directional signs, dry mount and laminate instructional materials, bind periodicals. They shelve books, compile booklists, tell stories, play games, help children find books, copy tapes, write overdue notices, process art prints and slides. Others might supervise the use of reading devices, operate closed circuit television equipment (to tape off air or operate video cameras and recorders in the classroom), tutor children who are not doing well in

group learning situations, visit classrooms and, in general, lend hands where extra hands are needed.[4]

Attracting helpers. Be alert for individuals who show an interest in the library and its programs, as well as those who have special talents needed by the library staff. You will soon find that library boosters are everywhere. They are the book lovers, study chairmen, teachers, mothers and fathers who read to their children, persons with previous library/media center experience and those who usually can be counted on to support the library whenever its programs come up for discussion at meetings.

Ask. Tell library boosters or persons with special talents that you need assistance and would like them to help. Quite often people only need to be asked.

Be specific. Individuals who might not wish to commit themselves to be on hand every Tuesday morning for a work session might be perfectly willing to take on a one-time specific assignment, such as a special program or event. Others rather like a small, repetitive task they feel comfortable doing week after week. Define exactly what is needed.

Praise. Thank helpers often to show your appreciation. This makes them receptive to being asked again. Invite them to attend the next library committee meeting as a visitor. Encourage them to make suggestions. As they become more involved with the programs and plans, they are apt to become regular helpers.

Rev. Gerald Kennedy says that a good administrator remembers that persons have needs, too. He believes that (a) everyone can do something (sometimes it is rather difficult to find just what a person can do, but we must keep on searching), (b) everyone wants to do something (the Reverend may not know this exactly but most criticism comes from people on the outskirts and not actively engaged in some part of the labor), and (c) everyone needs to do something (the most miserable people in the world are those with no obligations and no demands on them).[5]

Screening volunteers. In order to make a match between

the skill level of a person and the requirements of a job, the librarian needs to know something about the person. Find out what each volunteer *can* do, *likes* to do, and is *willing* to do.

Everyone wants to work the circulation desk, according to Winifred Brown of New York City's first centralized volunteer agency. She offers the following advice: "An in-depth interview with a prospective volunteer is crucial. . . . Be frank in specifying just what duties and responsibilities the job entails. . . Write volunteer job descriptions. . . Give prestige to your volunteers. . . Keep records useful in recognizing volunteer achievements and publicize your volunteer effort."[6]

Job Descriptions

What does the staff do? Each person on the library committee and staff should know exactly what is expected of him or her. Write out job descriptions that identify the general responsibilities and the specific duties of each assignment.

Library committee. The library committee acts as an administrative and advisory group to oversee development of the library ministry. Specific duties include:

- Establishing goals and policies for library operation
- Deciding how much funding is needed, arranging to obtain it, and overseeing the expenditure
- Arranging a suitable location for the library
- Appointing a librarian
- Encouraging use of the library and promoting goodwill

The *chairman* of the library committee acts as the official channel of communication between the library and the governing bodies of the congregation. Specific duties of the chairman include presiding over meetings of the committee, preparing the agenda, reporting to the administrative groups of the parent organization—to ask for funding, location, etc. or to report on the progress and needs of the library—evaluating the performance of the librarian, and communicating with the congregation to determine information needs and to evaluate the library's effectiveness in fulfilling these needs.

Members of the library committee include representatives of the major activities of the church or synagogue. These persons are responsible for advising the committee of special informational needs of the groups they represent, recommending additions in the way of materials or services, and keeping their own groups informed of the resources and services available.

The *Secretary* of the library committee is responsible for keeping the records of meetings. Specific duties include taking minutes of meetings, preparing copies for distribution and for a permanent file in the library, and notifying members of approaching meetings by placing a notice in the Sunday bulletin or by a telephone call or a mailed card.

The *Treasurer* of the library committee is responsible for receiving and disbursing all funds earned by the committee, received as gifts, or granted as budget allotments. Specific duties include arranging to receive amounts budgeted by the parent organization and other groups such as the women's society or the day school, checking and paying invoices, keeping accurate accounts and other records, reporting at committee meetings, and monitoring expenditures and obligations against budget balances. Sometimes the committee treasurer also acts as the library's purchasing agent.

The *Purchasing Agent* is responsible for buying all library materials and equipment. Specific duties include identifying sources and discounts, placing orders, keeping records of same, receiving the material, and verifying invoices for payment. The purchasing agent often keeps a record of previous orders, especially for items that will need to be reordered at a later date.

The *Librarian* is responsible for running the library and for carrying out policies established by the library committee in regard to organizing the collection, selecting and ordering materials, accepting gifts, circulating and/or using materials, and special services. Specific duties include recruiting and training a staff of helpers, establishing procedures, and overseeing the care of materials and equipment. The librarian works with the committee to promote use of the library and its services, provides reference and reader advisory service, and maintains accurate records of library use. The librarian also nurtures good working relationships with other libraries in the area in order to promote use of materials through interlibrary loan and to serve the broader community as well as the local congregation.

"The church librarian cannot be a substitute Sunday school teacher and also perform the services that the librarian needs to be offering," advise June and Earl Dorn.[7] In short, the librarian should not be expected to do a lot of other tasks around the church during the times when the library is functioning. This needs to be understood by everyone.

The job description for a paid librarian needs to be quite specific. Here is an example:

Position: CHURCH LIBRARIAN

Reports to: Library committee

Description (Summary):

As church librarian, is reponsible for operating the church library with policy guidance from the library committee. Selects material, organizes the collection and makes it available for use. Coordinates with the ministerial staff and various church departments to make the church library a ministry that serves the entire church. Works along with and helps to train the volunteer library staff. Promotes use of the library and prepares reports. (12 hours per week)

Responsibilities:

1. Keeps a record of spending for the library.

2. Decides on what books and supplies are needed for the library.

3. Meets with the library staff at an appointed time each week and assigns special duties.

4. Takes care of processing of books and all mechanics of the library, supervising the work of the library assistants. Keeps up-to-date files and records.

5. Is familiar with the general content of the library, including audiovisual materials.

6. Is on hand on Sunday mornings to answer requests for information, such as reference questions, file sign-out cards, receive returned books, place sign-out cards in them and reshelve, check in and out audiovisual materials.

7. Periodically weeds out books in need of repair, replacement, or discard.

8. Hosts groups, such as church school classes, who visit the library to learn what is available and how items may be checked out. Visits classes for the same purpose.

9. Promotes use of the library, by reviewing books and other materials for groups, setting up displays, arranging bulletin boards, writing publicity for the church paper, etc.

10. Attends meetings of the library committee and others, as required.

11. Develops good working relations with the ministries of the church.

12. Informs the library committee of problems and needs and submits an annual report which includes records of circulation, number of books, and other media materials added (by classification), and amount spent during the year.

13. Works in coordination with assistant librarians, such as the cataloger and the multimedia librarian.

Cataloger. An assistant librarian might take care of cataloging all the materials. For example, Mrs. Herbert M. Payne of the First Lutheran Church Library in Ellicott City, Maryland, reports: "We have two active librarians; one who reviews and purchases books and gives good general assistance to patrons; the other who is responsible for cataloging, developing and keeping our records."[8] The library, which serves 234 registered borrowers, has 500 books and a collection of pictures, periodicals and films.

The responsibilities of the cataloger are to prepare materials for storage, circulation and use, and to maintain a record of all materials in the collection. Specific duties include accessioning, classifying, preparing catalog cards, filing, labeling, pasting, affixing jacket covers, keeping statistics of additions and withdrawals, and compiling a regular list of new additions. Catalogers often develop procedures manuals for processing, to record established policies and routines. These are handy references and aid in training new helpers. A good example of a procedures manual is *Cataloging Books Step By Step* (Bryn Mawr, PA: Church & Synagogue Library Association, 1977).

Audiovisual Librarian, or Media Specialist. The responsibilities of this job are to help build a collection of nonprint materials, prepare them for circulation, and encourage their use. Duties include suggesting additions and withdrawals, scheduling use, providing help (a projectionist or teaching how to use), maintaining the equipment, materials, and facilities for a learning center, working with the church school-teachers to coordinate activities, and keeping abreast of materials outside the library which might be available for loan, rental, or purchase. Reports to the librarian on progress, problems, and future plans.

Children's Librarian, or Church School Librarian. The responsibilities are to guide and nurture growth and development of the children's collection. Duties include keeping abreast of what is needed, suggesting additions or withdrawals, stimulating use of the collection such as preparing booklists, talking to children's groups, setting up story hours, distributing bookmarks, etc. and working with teachers in the church school to coordinate some of these activities. If a church school librarian, the responsibilities are broader: represents the church school on the library committee. Duties include consulting with the superintendents and teachers, culling through curriculum materials for suggested purchases for all age levels, preparing booklists, etc. A church school librarian also advises workers and pupils of all ages what materials and services are available to support the teaching program.

Help in various areas can be useful and appreciated. Consider people who might assume responsibility in the following areas.

Circulation: Keep records of the number of books and other materials that go out into circulation. This helps to determine use of the library. If the count is kept by classification number and type of media, it also tells the librarian which subjects or types of material are most heavily used. For example, at one time we discovered that the circulation of children's books almost equalled that of adults even though the collection was one quarter the size; the following year a greater proportion of children's books were added to the collection. The person undertaking this task might also be assigned the responsibility of receiving returned books, shelving—"reading the shelves"—to make sure books are in the right order, notifying borrowers of overdue material, maintaining a waiting list for popular items, and assisting in taking periodic inventories of the collection.

Gifts: Sort, accept or reject gifts that are appropriate additions to the library, affix book plates, send note of thanks to donors, notify donors when the book is ready for circulation. Maintain an album listing all gifts to the library. Prepare reports to the librarian about gifts received.

Mending and repair: Mend and repair books and other materials as needed. Suggest items for rebinding, replacement, or discard. One project we undertook along this line was to gather a crew of workers and mend all the church hymnals in one session. Materials include permanent mending tape for torn pages and for fastening book jacket covers, library paste for pasting or glueing loose sections and book pockets, mystic tape for reinforcing spines of books, perforated adhesive cloth for use when a board cover loosens from the first paper page of the book, art gum eraser for cleaning marks on pages, and book cleaner for brightening up the covers of books.

Pamphlet and clipping file: Develop and maintain a file of pamphlets and clippings suitable for use, to supplement the book collection. Mount clippings, if needed. Prepare, mark, stamp, and file materials in accordance with established procedures.

Periodicals: Order and receive all periodicals and maintain records of same. Subscribe to periodicals as requested by the librarian and keep subscriptions current. Report any gifts. Record issues as they come in and notify the librarian if an anticipated issue is not received, so a claim can be filed with the publisher or subscription agent. Stamp and file periodicals according to established procedures.

Picture file: Develop a file of pictures suitable for use in the education program, on bulletin boards, for devotional programs, etc. Receive and prepare for use the pictures and picture kits ordered for the church school. Go through old magazines, calendars, and other sources for suitable pictures. Mount or frame pictures as required and file or store as appropriate.

Publicity: Keep the library before the people of the congregation so they will know the facilities, resources, and services the library offers and special programs the library sponsors. This includes publicizing (in the newsletter or Sunday bulletin, posted, or otherwise distributed) new additions, gifts, library milestones, and special events. It also might include responsibility for changing the bulletin boards and setting up exhibits in the library display case or elsewhere.

Shut-ins: Take books and other materials to shut-ins by personal visits, mail, or messenger.

Library duty: Libraries often operate with honor-charging systems, but there are times when assistance is needed by the users. One or more staff members could be assigned for duty in the library at regularly scheduled hours.

Sarah Wallace, speaking at an annual conference of the Church and Synagogue Library Association said, "A collection may be rich and its housing all that is desired, but the library will still lack effectiveness if the librarian is not there—a librarian who knows the collection, who understands people and cares about them, who can interpret their vague and sometimes stumbling requests into the need that lies behind them, who knows how to meet that need with friendship and understanding and the right book."[9]

If the librarian cannot be present when the library is at its busiest or needs help to handle all the people, other staff members familiar with the collection should be scheduled to help. Normally, the librarian will handle this scheduling, post it or announce the current assignments at a meeting of the staff.

The person on duty in the library generally is responsible for:

Circulation: Help patron charge out materials. Record circulation for statistics and file cards in circulation file. Replace cards in returned books. File books back on the shelf.

Reference service: Be there. Answer questions and help people find material for general reading, or for a specific topic. Keep a record of inquiries for use in future collection development.

Training

New volunteers have to become familiar with the library, its policies, and its resources. In one library, each new recruit is assigned to an old-timer with experience. The two work as a team during the training period. The experienced helper suggests when the newcomer is familiar enough with the routines to "go it alone."

A slide-tape orientation program was prepared by a high school librarian in San Jose, California, to introduce students to the library.[10] This technique could be equally effective with new volunteers.

Associations and services. One of the most helpful ways to train yourself, and others, for the job is to visit other libraries, to get acquainted with other individuals working with books and library materials and ask questions as you observe various processes and problems. Most public and school librarians are very cooperative in sharing information. Most congregational librarians are even eager to do so.

The interdenominational Church Library Council in the greater Washington, D.C. area grew from seven church librarians getting together to share ideas. Today the Council has chapters in the District of Columbia and surrounding counties. The members meet in small local groups but get together quarterly to invite speakers and explore mutual interests. Since they meet at various churches and synagogues, they get to see other libraries.

The national library associations often have local chapters, publish newsletters, bulletins and guides, and sponsor conferences and workshops. See the Resource Section for a list of library associations and denominational groups which offer church library services such as these.

Workshops and conferences. Library associations and denominational groups, on request, often will send a qualified teacher to set up a library workshop for an individual church or a group of churches and/or synagogues in a local area. These workshops can be tailored to fit individual needs and give an entire library committee one or more days of concentrated instruction. The costs generally include the teacher's expenses.

Two major denominational services hold week-long workshops twice a year. The Church Library Department of the Southern Baptist Convention holds them at Ridgecrest, North

Carolina, and Glorietta, New Mexico. Cokesbury Church Library Association holds them at Lake Junaluska, Greensboro, North Carolina, and Mt. Sequoyah, Fayetteville, Arkansas.

Local bookstores, councils of churches, public libraries, clubs, associations, schools, and groups of churches sometimes sponsor library conferences, workshops, roundtables, institutes, symposia, and similar group meetings which offer opportunities to learn library skills.

The Jewish Library Association of Greater Philadelphia held a series of eight classes on librarianship one spring. It was designed for volunteers, and church as well as synagogue librarians were invited to participate.[11]

Chapters of the Church and Synagogue Library Association often sponsor workshops. These might include sessions on starting a library, basic library techniques, book repair, multimedia resources, book selection, and promoting the library.

When there is evidence of need for holding a workshop training program, locate a sponsor and then help with the planning. Any learning experience should be tailored to fit the needs of the individuals who are expected to attend. A useful manual that gives helpful hints for the workshop committee and chairman as well as the leader of a session and provides sample programs, forms, and materials is *Workshop Planning*, 2nd ed. (CSLA Guide No. 3), Church and Synagogue Library Association, Box 1130, Bryn Mawr, PA 19010. 1979.

Correspondence courses. The University of Utah, Division of Continuing Education, has developed a correspondence study program for church and synagogue librarianship. This course, available to anyone interested in church library work, focuses on the physical facilities of the library, the staff you work with, and choosing, ordering, cataloging, and classification of books and materials for the library. Yearly budget, library hours, and involvement outside the local scene also are covered. The course consists of fifteen lessons and an optional final exam. The fee is a modest one. For more information about this course and several others on librarianship in general write to Independent Study Department, University of Utah, 1152 Annex, Salt Lake City, UT 84112.[12]

Formal training. Although traditional library training is available in general, some colleges and universities are beginning to offer credit courses and seminars for church librarians specifically.

Elsie Lehman, curriculum librarian at Eastern Mennonite College, Harrisonburg, Virginia, led a church librarians' seminar at college. The program centered on establishing and developing a church library and integrating it with the program of the church. Twenty-three librarians attended and received half a unit credit in the Continuing Education Program of the college.[13]

The Congregational Librarians' Association of British Columbia persuaded Douglas College to sponsor a night school course entitled "Theological Libraries, a Short Course for Library Workers in Religious Institutions." The course covered basic library skills, including selection and promotion.[14]

Baylor University, Waco, Texas, offered a new course in "Administration of Church Libraries" at its Summer 1978 session.[15]

Look for schools in your area that offer continuing education classes. Inquire if they already have, or would consider having, a formal training program for library volunteers. Since standard library procedures are applicable to all types of libraries, such a program would be valuable for volunteers in church and synagogue libraries as well as public and school libraries.

Motivation and Encouragement

What makes an individual volunteer want to work in a church library? A love of books? Yes. The pleasure of socializing with congenial colleagues? Yes. The satisfaction of doing something worthwhile? Indeed. Then, why is there such a turnover in volunteer help? Some turnover is inevitable—people move away, go back to work for a salary, and sometimes have periods of failing health. Other turnover could be avoided by leadership sensitive to the needs and personalities of individuals.

Librarians who manage to attract and hold a loyal staff over a period of time generally are enthusiastic, knowledgeable about their work, and considerate of other individuals. They make every effort to:

- Provide a working environment that is comfortable and in which everyone can feel at ease.
- Give each staff member a responsibility that is his or her own—no matter how small—but make sure it is within the person's abilities to perform. Provide adequate training.
- Encourage the staff to make suggestions and participate in developing library plans.
- Let them know, as often as necessary, that their contribution is valuable and appreciated.

Appreciation. To attract and hold a volunteer staff, you must find ways to show appreciation. Volunteers, especially, need this kind of encouragement. Even though they believe the work they are doing is worthwhile, they like to have their contribution recognized. Effective ways to do this might be: (a) Tell a helper whenever a job has been well done, (b) record your appreciation in writing, at least once a year, (c) name your helpers in the reports and speeches you present to groups, publish in the bulletin, or post for the congregation to see, (d) encourage your pastor, priest, or rabbi to say a word about the library and its staff at an official meeting of the congregation or from the pulpit, (e) plan an event to honor the volunteers, when you can call attention to their years of service (give awards if you like) and note the accomplishments of the staff, or (f) arrange a special Sunday for library recognition. Ask to say a few words about the library and its staff to the assembled congregation. Keep in mind that the attitudes of the staff will determine in large measure the kind of library you have.

6

ORDERING MATERIALS

When we were starting our church library, I became a familiar figure at the local public library. As often as I could I sought out Mary Dulany, the head librarian. She knew all the answers and was a never-ending source of encouragement.

"Where do you buy your books?" she asked me one day. I must have looked startled, calling to mind our collection of hand-me-downs from the church, gifts from well-meaning parishioners, and purchases made by church school helpers "for the library."

"We have money only for supplies," I confessed, "but we should be able to buy some new books as soon as the new church budget year begins." Then, noting the smile on her face and the light in her eye, I asked, "What did you have in mind?"

"Why don't you try Cucumber," she replied.

"Cucumber!" I echoed.

"Cucumber Bookshop," she repeated. "It's not what it sounds like." She then told me how the Cucumber Bookshop began as a little retail shop in the suburban Washington, D.C. community of Bethesda, Maryland. One of its memorable features was a red-painted wheelbarrow which leaned against the side of the building. This was a bargain barrel of slightly soiled books marked "wilted cucumbers." The small retail store grew, the wheelbarrow disappeared, and the store gradually became a wholesale business.

"Why don't you go over there and talk with Mr. Carpenter," Mary suggested. "He'll probably give you a discount, too. It might not be as much as ours, because you are a smaller library, but I am sure he will allow you a library discount." I thanked her and determined to visit Cucumber very soon.

Most beginning librarians find out about dealers and discounts from someone else who knows. Then they learn from experience how best to order their own library supplies, books, and other materials.

Have a Purchasing Plan

Whenever our library received a sizable gift or a budget allowance, my first thought was how much I could buy. Then, as shopping began, I tried to figure out how much I could save. Over the years, selecting and ordering materials and supplies made me more conscious of prices, discounts, sources, and service. I recommend the following simple shopping plan:

1. Know in advance what you want to buy. Make a shopping list. Include books, other media materials, and supplies. Review your collection, current curriculum guides, "hot topic" discussions among the congregation, and your "wish list."
2. Check your budget. Make sure the total price of your shopping list is within the range of what you can afford to spend.
3. Select a source. Choose more than one if necessary. Look for good service and/or a library discount.
4. Be businesslike in your dealings. Know how to place orders, how to keep records, how to receive or return purchases, and how to verify invoices for payment.

Purchasing Guidelines

Guidelines for purchasing are a must. Sometimes individuals become enthusiastic about books or other materials they see, perhaps at a conference, and, on impulse, buy them for the library. You need to keep control over what is ordered. Eugene Neithold suggests the following general rules:

1. Designate one person to serve as a purchasing agent.
2. No person will incur an expense on behalf of the church

expecting to be reimbursed unless approved by the individual responsible for purchasing.

3. No person will purchase an item with a personal check (or cash) expecting to be reimbursed unless approved by the individual reponsible for purchasing.
4. Purchasing files may be maintained which consist of vendor literature (catalogs, etc.) and memos from others concerning their experiences with specific vendors.
5. Purchases of over (dollar amount) should be paid by check.
6. Large expenditures, for equipment for example, require the approval of (person's name or position), if not specified in the budget.[1]

Tax-exempt status. Churches and synagogues normally have tax-exempt status in the United States. One of the benefits this provides is they do not have to pay sales tax on purchases, when they display to the dealer their tax-exempt identification number.

Ask if your organization has a tax-exempt number and, if so, if you may use it in purchasing materials for the library. Some stewards of church affairs guard this privilege zealously, lest the number be used to make purchases other than for the church. Such permission is easier to obtain when the church is assured that only one person will be in a position to use it and will use it responsibly.

Library Supplies

Along with the exciting thought of getting new books and other materials—gifts as well as purchases—you will need to think about the supplies required to catalog and care for them.

Library supply houses. Specialized library supplies normally are obtained from library supply houses. These include items such as catalog cards, book cards and pockets, labels, book supports, periodical binders, library forms, binding tape, microfilm readers, etc. They usually must be ordered by mail from a dealer specializing in library supplies. See Resources for a list of some library suppliers. Additional sources are listed in the "Annual Buyers' Guide" printed in the *Library Journal* each September 1 (available at most public libraries).

Supply houses also offer specialty products, such as book-carrying bags, circulation control systems, display kits, electric marking pens, "Library Aide" buttons, and filing containers for all sorts of multimedia materials. Available products are listed in the dealer's catalog, often with color illustrations as well as detailed descriptions. When dealing with library supply houses, it is wise to order a six-month supply. If the library has the storage space, order enough to last one year.

Local stationery stores. General office supplies can be obtained from local stationery stores, which normally do not carry the specialized library supplies. For these general supplies, the local store provides the advantage of personal contact. You can see and evaluate the supplies before you purchase, and question the sales clerk and make exchanges, if needed, with relative ease. Supplies that typically are available at stationery stores are typewriter ribbons, bond paper, paper clips, pencils, manila folders, etc. These need not be stockpiled in quantity. They can be purchased as needed.

For information about material required for cataloging, and commercial cataloging services, see *Cataloging Made Easy; How to Organize Your Congregation's Library* (New York, NY: Seabury Press, 1978).

Book Sources

Books are available from a variety of sources. Purchases normally are made (a) direct from the publisher, (b) from a denominational publishing house, (c) from a retail bookstore, or (d) from a wholesale book dealer.

Publishers. If you purchase direct from a publisher, you can expect from 10 percent to 25 percent library discount on most books, a catalog of available books and, usually, postage paid delivery. However, books ordered from publishers might require several individual letters of request, damaged books must be returned by mail for refund or replacement, and you receive invoices from many sources using many different systems of accounting.

Denominational outlets. If you purchase from a denominational outlet, such as a denominational publishing house, you are certain to find a larger stock of denominational literature. Sometimes this is the only source for official church items such as hymnals, books of worship, etc. Many denominational publishers distribute colorful, illustrated catalogs which help in the selection of books, and sometimes allow books to be taken on consignment or on approval. However, the library discount generally is smaller (perhaps 15 percent to 20 percent), and you pay the postage for delivery. Sometimes, however, the library billing gets mixed up with the regular billing that goes to the church for other things and the discount is lost, and service sometimes is slow.

Retail bookstore. If you purchase from a retail bookstore, try to find one that specializes in religious literature. From this source, chances are that many of the books you want will be carried in stock. That means you can see the books before you buy. Much can be learned from the attractive formats, jacket blurbs, and glances at the illustrations, print, and contents. However, the retail dealer offers the smallest discount—10 percent or 15 percent, if any—and often will charge a fee if asked to order an unusual book or to make deliveries.

Wholesale book dealer. If you purchase from a wholesale book dealer, you probably will get the best library discount, as much as 25 percent to 33-1/3 percent on standard trade books. This provides a single source of billing, as well. If you are fortunate enough to have a wholesale dealer in your own area, you also can pick up the books and sometimes see them before you buy. For a list of wholesale book dealers, see the annual *Literary Market Place* (New York, NY: R. R. Bowker Co.) which is available in most public libraries.

The larger wholesale book dealers do most of their business by mail. Those in metropolitan areas generally provide the best service and the most consistent discounts. They will try to supply almost any book in print, but if the book is not in stock in their warehouse the service is apt to be slower. They tend to accumulate orders for a single publisher in order to obtain the maximum discount. Wholesale dealers seldom issue a catalog and their stock of church or synagogue library books is apt to be small.

Standing orders. Certain books, such as almanacs, are revised annually. Others, such as the official hymnal, are revised at irregular intervals. Still others, such as volumes in a set, are issued over a period of time. You may be interested in making sure that you get the newest edition or the most recent volumes as they are published.

Ask your book dealers if they handle standing orders. If so, you can place an order for all future editions to be sent to you, along with the invoice, as they become available.

Keep a standing order file of your own, with estimated dates, new editions, or volumes expected to come out. If you have placed a standing order with your dealer, this will alert you to follow up if the book is not received. If you have been unable to place a standing order, your record will be a reminder to order the item when it is available.

Compare service. In summary, there is no single perfect source for buying books. If discounts are of greatest importance, find a wholesale dealer and allow a little extra time for deliveries. If promptness is what you need, order from the denominational outlet or the local religious bookstore. If personal contact is important—you want to see the books before you buy—stay with the local bookstore. If shopping by catalog is preferable, select your favorite publishers and write for their catalogs, even if some of these cost money. Decide the kind of service you need. Then, compare the various sources.

Periodical Subscriptions

Subscriptions to current periodicals may be placed directly with the publisher of each magazine. They also may be handled through a subscription agency.

Basic requirements. The biggest challenge in dealing with periodical subscriptions is keeping track of expiration and/ or renewal dates. A subscription that expires in December will need to be renewed before that date, perhaps in September or October, in order to maintain continuity of receipt. Allow sixty to ninety days for the paperwork on a subscription, or a renewal, to go through the publisher's or agency's record system. For this reason, publishers often start sending out renewal notices long before the subscription expires and, sometimes, long after the renewal has been sent in. This can be very confusing and it is imperative that you keep good records of your own (see chapter 7, Keeping Track of Assets).

The second biggest challenge is keeping track of the expected issues when they are due to arrive. A new issue might normally be received at the beginning of the month. If so, report it promptly when yours is not received within a week or two of that time; this is a claim. Another copy of the missing issue will be sent to you at no extra charge. If you wait several months before making a claim for missing issues, the publisher might very well be out of stock.

Dealing direct. The advantage of dealing with a publisher is that you have direct contact to resolve problems of subscription dates or claims. However, if the publisher has an automated system of handling subscriptions, this direct contact might well be with a computer and not a human being. Also, if you subscribe to a number of magazines, you need to correspond with a number of publishers, each with differences in the way they respond. You also will be handling a number of invoices of various sizes, shapes, and complexity.

Subscription agencies. A subscription agency will channel all your orders to the appropriate publishers and act as your agent in regard to renewals and claims. You have only one source to deal with and one invoice, which will list all your subscriptions, their cost, and date of expiration. They do save time and effort.

Multimedia Suppliers

Libraries are developing more and more as multimedia centers. Audiovisuals and other nonbook resources are becoming as important as books. Selection of the materials, and the equipment to use them, often determines the source from which they must be obtained.

What is available. Selection will be based on what is available and what is needed in the programs and by the parishioners. To find what is available, scan catalogs, read reviews and visit the vendors who specialize in multimedia materials.

Particularly useful are the catalogs and curriculum guides issued by denominations. They often recommend audiovisuals, such as filmstrips, cassette tapes and records, as well as other materials, such as maps, globes, teaching pictures, kits and games.

Reviews of multimedia materials can be found in periodicals, such as *Church & Synagogue Libraries* (Box 1130, Bryn Mawr, PA 19010) and *Media; Library Services Journal* (127 Ninth Avenue North, Nashville, TN 37234).

Church bookstores and similar retail outlets often carry multimedia materials for use in educational programs. Some even provide facilities where items such as filmstrips can be viewed before they are purchased.

Margaret Korty rates the *Audio-Visual Resources Guide* (9th edition edited by Nick Abrams, New York: Friendship Press, 1972) as "very useful in selection." She says this all-purpose source guide "gives ratings, summaries, age levels for films, filmstrips, slides, records, tapes and pictures."[2]

The National Information Center for Educational Media issues an *Index to Free Educational Material - Multimedia* (Los Angeles, CA: NICE/University of Southern California, 1978). This and other general selection tools quite often are available at public and school libraries.

Look to the denomination's communications division as a potential source for audiovisual materials about the beliefs and activities of your own faith. For example, Church Resources System (P.O. Box 990, Dallas, TX) is owned by seven Methodist Annual Conferences in Texas and New Mexico. It is operated by the Media Division of the United Methodist Communications Council which publishes a CRS *Update* newsletter. Along with items about media events, communications workshops, and services or equipment, are notices about available resources, such as "John Wesley: Practical Evangelist" (a 16mm film available from United Methodist Filmservice, 1525 McGavrock Street, Nashville, TN 37203) and "Faith Alive Bible Stories" (a series of 14 cassettes which contain 56 stories in all, available from CRS).[3] Write to the communications division of your church or synagogue and ask for information about multimedia resource materials. Ask what they have and whether it is available for purchase or loan.

Equipment. It is difficult to think about audiovisual resources without thinking about the equipment needed to use it. Availability of the proper equipment controls selection and use of the material.

Edward Hingers says, "For the audiovisual librarian, faced with new and ever-changing technologies . . . the establishment and maintenance of good relationships with suppliers is of prime importance. When a reliable dealer is found, he is to be cherished. His role should continue before, during and after the sale."[4]

Good dealers will be invaluable in helping you make wise choices of equipment based on your own unique needs. They are in a position to suggest acceptable substitutes within your alloted budget. They also should be in a position to follow up with good service, if needed, after the sale is completed. From experience, good dealers know the advantages and disadvantages of almost any situation and will stand behind their advice.

Specific information about equipment is available from the manufacturer of the equipment, trade shows, and dealers. Many public libraries have useful guides, such as the *Audio-Visual Equipment Directory*, an annual publication of the National Audio-Visual Association, Inc. (3150 Spring Street, Fairfax, VA 22030).

From time to time repair services will be required. Investigate the services or facilities available in your area for repairing film, recording audio or video tapes and disks, affixing identifying leaders to film, making duplicates, etc. Most laboratories will examine a film free of charge and report what can or cannot be done with it. The same holds true for cleaning or repairing equipment.

Plan for equipment maintenance on a more or less regular schedule. This minimizes the surprises of equipment malfunctioning when you need it most.

Handling Orders

The procedures for ordering are fairly simple: choose what you want, select a source, place the order. Yet the actual handling of orders is not always without snags. Here are some hints to make it smoother and, therefore, produce the best results.

Cultivate good relations. Make trading with you a pleasant experience. For example, know pretty well what you want. Look up order information in advance. If you are ordering a book, have the correct title, publisher, and price. If more than one edition is available, specify the one you want—cloth or paperback, for example. Information about current books can be found in references kept on file in the public library and in your dealer's shop and may be consulted there. If you do not have the information, offer to look it up yourself.

Let it be known that you appreciate your dealer as a source of good books. William Gentz suggests that if you are dealing with publishers you learn to know the publishers by name and reputation, write to them, let your interests and needs be known, visit them if you can, and when you write about books send the publisher a copy.[5]

Put it in writing. Type or write out your order, even if you plan to deliver it in person. Leave the original with the dealer and keep a copy for yourself. List each title on a separate slip or card. This makes it easier for the dealer to separate the orders that cannot be filled from stock.

Single or multipart order forms are available for purchase from the library supply dealers (see Resources for list of dealers).

A Book Order Can Make Buying Much Easier

CLASS NO.	AUTHOR	
ACCESSION NO.	TITLE	
COPIES ORDERED		
DATE ORDERED	PLACE AND PUBLISHER	YEAR
FROM	EDITION OR SERIES	LIST
DATE RECEIVED	ILLUSTRATOR	NO. OF COPIES
COST	DEPT. FOR WHICH RECOMMENDED	REVIEWED
L.C. OR WILSON CARD	TEACHER	
HIGHSMITH 46-183		

File your copy of the order in a pending order file. Be sure it shows the date on which the order was placed and by whom. Some librarians keep two copies in the suspense file— one under the title and the other under the date of the order, which makes it easier to pull out the orders that are overdue.

Follow up on the order. Find out how long it should take for your order to be filled, or estimate from your past experience. After a reasonable time has elapsed, inquire about it. Provide a copy of the original order, if possible; this helps the vendor identify the item.

Check what you receive. As soon as an order is received, check the pending order file. Be sure that what is received is what you ordered. Then look it over for possible flaws.

All materials should be checked for flaws as soon as received. The best way to check a book is to open it properly and collate the pages.

To open a book properly, place the spine of the book on a flat surface and open just the front and back cover, with the pages of the book still upright. Open a few pages from the front and a few pages from the back and press down along the inside margin. A teacher friend of mine calls this "shaking hands with the book." Repeat this until you reach the center of the book. This allows the binding to stretch gradually and keeps the spine from cracking.

To collate a book, go through the book page by page and be alert for misprinted pages, skipped pages, loose sections, or other imperfections in printing or binding. Uncut pages should be cut apart with a letter opener or other sharp object to avoid making a jagged tear which usually results from using your finger. Imperfect copies should be returned for replacement.

Acceptable copies should be marked "received" on the order card, with the date and the price to be paid. The book then is ready to be turned over to the cataloger for accessioning into the collection. (See chapter 7 Keeping Track of Assets.)

Pay the invoice promptly. Sometimes the invoice for an order is enclosed with the shipment. Other times it comes in separately—either before or after shipment is received. Hold the invoice until the order arrives and is accepted. Then, mark the invoice "received," with date and initials, and see to it that the invoice is paid promptly.

Procedures for the payment of invoices vary within organizations. Find out how this is to be done in your church/ synagogue. Write out these practices and follow them.

Book Fairs and Consignment Sales

Book fairs are fun. You can select a group of attractive new books and other materials, order them on consignment, offer them for sale, return any that are not sold (as long as they are still in good condition), and make a profit besides. Information about book fairs can be found in books such as *Getting the Books Off the Shelves; Making the Most of Your Congregation's Library* (New York: Hawthorn Books, 1975). There are practical ways to make handling consignment sales easier:

Act as the vendor's agent. When you accept a consignment of books, you really become the vendor's agent. You will be expected to look after the books, keep records straight, pay for those which are sold and return in shelf condition those which are not. Your "commission" for doing this is the allowable library discount on all the books that are sold.

Select a good source. Not all dealers allow books to go out on consignment. Investigate sources available and select the one which has the best selection for your purposes, allows the best discount, and offers the best service. Ask other librarians who have had experience with book sales and take advantage of their advice.

Keep records straight. Make sure that all books selected for consignment are accurately recorded on the invoice with the proper retail price. Check the boxes carefully against the invoices when you unpack. If the retail price is not clearly shown on the book, write it on a small pressure-sensitive, self-adhesive, label. Place this label on the book where it can be seen but will not damage the book when it is taken off.

When unsold books are to be returned for credit, make sure they get back to the dealer promptly and in *good condition* for sale as new books. If possible, enclose a list of the books being returned.

Renting and Borrowing Materials

Films, filmstrips, cassettes, records, audiovisual equipment and exhibits often can be borrowed or rented for short-term use from sources outside the library.

Locate sources. Public libraries are a good source for both multimedia materials and equipment. Some may charge a small fee for use of equipment, but these circulating-materials services generally are free.

The Hyattsville Branch of the Prince George's County, Maryland, Memorial Library lends reproductions of famous paintings and records of all types. "Talking books" for persons with limited sight or any other handicap that makes reading difficult or impossible are supplied by the Library of Congress, which also lends playing equipment to eligible users. The county libraries in various parts of the country coordinate and supplement this Library of Congress service and the services are provided without charge.[6]

The Hennepin County, Minnesota, Library received a National Association of Counties award in 1979 for its three-year-old chemical dependency film program, which had reached more than 6,000 individuals in retirement homes, community groups, churches, and schools. The library loaned the film free and provided the services of a trained volunteer to lead discussions and answer questions about chemical dependency.[7]

Since more than a million American households now own videocassette recorders, libraries nationwide are circulating materials in Betamax, VHS, and 3/4-inch U-matic formats. The Chicago Public Library announced plans to obtain 300 videotapes for loan. Likewise, after conducting an experiment in circulating videotapes, the San Francisco Public Library Communications Center started a permanent circulating VHS collection.[8]

The lending of media equipment is a part of the service program of many public libraries. When twenty-one public city or county libraries throughout the nation were surveyed, ten responded that they are circulating or renting a variety of audiovisual hardware, ranging from cassette players to portable public address systems. The most popular equipment included super 8mm, 16mm, slide and filmstrip projectors, reel-to-reel recorders, cassette players and player/recorders, overhead and opaque projectors, and screens. Several libraries reported that they circulate microfilm readers and printers, portable microfiche readers, and video cameras.[9]

Religious bookstores and denominational services are other sources. *Media: Library Services Journal* reviews filmstrips and recordings that are available for purchase through the Baptist bookstores. It also reviews motion pictures which can be rented from Baptist film centers. Prices are included.[10]

Other sources for nonprint materials are local councils of

churches, national associations, and the federal government's National Audiovisual Center (National Archives & Records Service, Washington, D.C. 20409).

Copying and Copyright

Copying machines are all around us these days. They are readily available in public libraries, hotels, and many offices. It is easy to copy printed materials. With the growing accessibility of audio and video recorders, it also is becoming easy to copy tape cassettes and TV programs as well as live choir music and other programs which might be based on copyrighted works.

Librarians, especially, need to be aware of the implications of copying copyrighted materials—when it is allowed under the law and when it is not.

Copyright law. A new copyright law went into effect in January 1978.[11] Under the new provisions, all original works of authorship can be registered for copyright whether they are published or not, as long as they are recorded in tangible form, such as a typed copy, a photo record, or a tape recording. If copyright protection is granted by the U.S. Copyright Office, the work may not be copied without prior approval of the copyright holder. Permission often requires payment of a royalty fee, but sometimes it is given free of charge.

"Fair use" copying. The new law recognizes the "fair use" concept, which allows copying to be done for purposes such as criticism, comment, news reporting, teaching (including multiple copies for classroom use), and for scholarship or research, without obtaining prior permission from the copyright holder. At the same time, the law specifically limits its use. For example, such copying must be reasonable, not harmful to the rights of the owner, and not detrimental to the potential market or value of the copyrighted work. Much remains to be ironed out in the interpretation. Fair use does not extend to the copying of sheet music and other works of art or to audio or video recordings which are copyrighted. So, when in doubt, write for permission.

Recordings. Some audio and video recordings are not copyrighted and, therefore, are not covered by the law. J. Kevin Dougherty points out that news broadcasts are outside the copyright law and may be copied. Sports broadcasts, dramas and editorial type programs often fall within the realm of copyright and may not be copied. In regard to the use of cassette recordings in schools, he says, "My rule of thumb is, if my copy is cheating you (the copyright holder) out of income, that's wrong. That's an infringement. But, bits and pieces of music or a documentary may be used in a classroom as a one-shot use—for instructional purposes—as long as you are not going to commercialize it and reap financial benefit from it."[12]

7

KEEPING TRACK OF ASSETS

Our screened porch is located high above ground, surrounded by tree branches. As we sat there one day, a cardinal began building a nest in the branches of a tree. First one twig. Then another. Each time the familiar chirp signaled her arrival with her mate and yet another twig. Each time she paused at the edge of the nest, looked it over carefully, and then dropped the twig in just the right spot. She hopped into the nest, snuggled into it, rearranged a few twigs, and flew off again. Day by day the nest took shape and one day she settled in to stay. During the brief periods she left the nest, we could see three whitish eggs with shades of brown. When she returned, she would pause at the edge of the nest to survey her assets. It seemed as though she were counting — one, two, three — to make sure they were all there and in the right place. Then, with an attitude of satisfaction and contentment, she settled her soft, feathery body over them to keep them warm and safe. Her mate was always nearby to distract intruders with his bright red plumage and loud chirping song. They were good managers and good stewards of their possessions.

Acquiring Resources

Like the cardinal, we gradually accumulate a nest egg of resources. When books and other materials are collected, a good steward will keep track of what is received, where it came from and its value. A good manager also will see that these assets are properly protected and cared for, cataloged and arranged for easy use.

Accessioning. Most moderately sized libraries use an Accession Book to keep track of material added to the collection. This is a loose-leaf binder with pages numbered from 1 to 49 and 50 to 99. As each new book is received, it is recorded in order of its arrival. The number beside the entry is the accession number, which is assigned to that book for life. It is a unique number and is never re-assigned to another book, even if the book is lost and replaced. Therefore, it can be inscribed in the book as an identifying copy number. Each new entry in the accession book is dated, so you know when that book was acquired. Other information recorded includes the author, title, publisher, date of publication, source, cost, and remarks. Under remarks, the donor can be identified if the book is a gift. This accession book tells you how many books were added to the collection, when, and their value.

Other media materials often are given accession numbers in separate number ranges. For example, a series of numbers are prefaced by a symbol that designates the type of media: FS-1 (filmstrips), SL-1 (slidesets), etc.

Periodicals check-in. A record of each periodical subscription can be maintained on a periodicals check-in card. These are available from library supply houses and normally come in two styles. One is lined by day, to record receipt of daily and weekly issues. The other is lined by month, for monthly, bimonthly, quarterly or irregular issues.

When a new subscription is placed, fill out a record card. File it by title, preferably in the shelf list file (see below). As each new issue is received, check the appropriate box on the record card. You will see at a glance if an issue is missing that should have been received. This is a reminder to send in a claim for the missing issue.

Arrangement. How materials are arranged on the shelf will determine how easy it is to browse or to find specific items when needed. A classification scheme provides a consistent blueprint for the arrangement. A card catalog provides an index, or road map, which tells where on the shelf specific items can be found. Additional information on arrangement, classification schemes, and cataloging can be found in *Cataloging Made Easy* (New York, NY: Seabury Press, 1978).

Shelf list. A record of material as it is filed on the shelf is called the shelf list. Most libraries use an additional catalog card and file it under the classification number.

On the shelf list card you probably will want to record the accession number. When a second copy is added to the collection, add that accession number to the same shelf list card. This shelf list card then will indicate the number of copies you have in the collection. (See later section in Inventory.)

Record of gifts. Many libraries like to keep an album which lists all gifts received and the names of the donors. Denominational supply houses have "In Remembrance" albums. These generally are handsome, loose-leaf albums with red cover embossed in gold. The pages are printed with space for the name of donors, the gift presented, and the person in whose memory or honor it was given.

A record of all gifts is more than just a "nice thing to do." It is an important part of your organization's business. In *Church Business Policies Outlined,* Eugene Neithold describes the gift receipt process, the valuation of donated items, donation of time worked for the church, and recognition of offerings by church members. In this book he also provides examples of forms for keeping such records.[1]

Using the Collection

If you want your collection to be used to full advantage, be sure the material is up-to-date and of interest to potential users. Keep the room clean and attractive. In this way you encourage resources to be used.

Circulation. When my son was a little boy, he had a toy that held his interest like no other. It came equipped with red wooden balls and a hammer. He would place the ball on the hole at the top, bang it with the hammer and the ball would go rolling down through the box and out the other end. This was repeated over and over and gave him a great deal of satisfaction. As a librarian, the ball running through its course over and over again reminded me of circulating books. Books are taken out of the library, read and returned, taken out, read and returned, again and again. Unlike the red balls, books have an individual identity. Records are kept. When an individual title is not on the shelf, the librarian should know where it is located (perhaps on display) or who has it (in circulation). Many libraries provide a book card held in a pocket inside the back cover of each book that circulates. This book card provides an easy record which stays with the book while it is on the shelf and remains with the librarian when it is not on the shelf.

Rules. Even the simplest of "games" need rules. Post simple how-to instructions with the rules for borrowing materials. The Library Committee is responsible for these rules, which include who may borrow, what may be borrowed, how to take out books and other materials, and when and where to return them.

Hours. The more hours the library is open, the greater convenience it will be for users. The library of the Bethesda United Methodist Church is never locked. It is open and available for use whenever the church itself is open. However, some libraries, for one reason or another, cannot remain open at all times. Quite often they post their hours and plan to have someone in attendance — especially before and after the regular worship services, and perhaps for major meetings during the week.

The First Presbyterian Church in Shreveport, Louisiana, is open every morning of the week. "The time between the Sunday service and church school account for its main business and circulation. An average of 200 books are checked out each week."[2]

Who may borrow. The librarian will want to maintain a system of records whereby both the readers and the material may be located at any time.

Some libraries — especially those who extend borrowing privileges to nonmembers — maintain a borrowers record as a means of identification. This can be a simple card with name, address, telephone number, and other useful information about the borrower — with the date the card was prepared. Such a file can serve two purposes. First, it simplifies locating borrowers when books are overdue. Second, it can become a useful reference on which to note the borrowers' reading habits, the kind of books they like, and their fields of interest.

What may be borrowed. Books that are not allowed to circulate usually are marked "Reference." Reference books are for use in the library and seldom go out except overnight.

Books that are allowed to circulate have a book pocket and book card in the book. This book card identifies the book and has spaces for date and borrower's name.

Periodicals often are allowed to circulate, but they seldom have a card and pocket pasted in the back. Instead, blank cards are provided on which the name and date of the periodical and who is taking it out can be written. Some libraries circulate only the back issues and keep the current issues on reserve to be read in the library.

Pamphlets, clippings, maps, and pictures often are charged out in the same way. A blank card is used to write what material is taken, the date, and by whom. In this way, several pamphlets, or pictures, may be charged on one card.

Audiovisual materials normally have a card and are charged out like books. If not, a blank card — or a charge sheet — is used to record number, title, date, and borrower's name.

Most materials in the library circulate for a standard period of time, such as two weeks, three weeks, or one month. A longer loan period means less clerical work in checking overdues, but it also means that material is absent from the shelves for a longer time.

Our library provides a "vacation loan" for people who are going away for the summer. All we ask is that they sign their name on the book card and indicate the date they expect to return from vacation.

Some things are in special demand. Even two weeks is too long a time for them to be out. Shorten the period of loan, when necessary, and call attention to this in some way — perhaps with a colored card in front of the book card indicating that the item is for 7-day loan only, or 3-day loan, or overnight.

Keep a list of waiting readers. Clip this list onto the book card. Notify the next reader on the list when the book again is available. Some libraries make a modest charge for "reserving" books because a postcard is sent to notify the waiting reader that it is being held for pick up.

How to borrow and return. A common practice in many libraries is to have the borrowers write their name and the date on the book card when they wish to check it out. The book card then is left in a well-marked box on the librarian's desk.

There should be a specifically identified place where books are to be returned. Preferably, this will be where the books will not be disturbed or put back on the shelf until the book card is taken out of the circulation file and slipped back into the book pocket. The Bethesda United Methodist Church library has a "Book Return" bin for this purpose which operates like a mailbox. Thus the returned books are protected until the librarian can retrieve them and replace the book cards.

Overdues and fines. The librarian's lament is, "How do I get books back when people keep them overdue?" No matter what the rules, some borrowers are certain to keep material past its due date. Therefore, you need a policy and procedure for handling overdues. Keep in mind that (a) your own records might be in error or (b) the borrower might have a reasonable need for continued use.

Check your records first. Look on the shelf to make sure the material has not been returned and inadvertently filed without its card.

Flag overdue material in the circulation file. After a reasonable time, send out notices in the form of a postcard or note, or contact the borrower by telephone or in person. If the due date has merely been overlooked, this reminder will be appreciated.

If the borrower really needs the material for a longer period, the system should be flexible enough to accommodate the need. For example, have a policy which can accommodate the need, such as a loan may be renewed as long as no one else is waiting to use the material.

Some libraries charge fines for overdue books, others do not. Since congregational libraries are special libraries serving specific congregations, often they do not.

The American Library Association's Library Administration Division, Circulation Services Section, studied fines and recommended that fines and penalties be eliminated. "In general they work (get the book back), but intimidate children, discourage them, punish them, and leave them reluctant to check out books."[3]

Jack W. Griffith, librarian of the Lewis Central High School, Council Bluffs, Iowa, suggests a "Free Week." "Set aside an occasional week when no fines will be charged on anything returned late. . . . Put up signs in the library and on doors and windows that can be read from outside." You might try announcing it in the congregation's newsletter[4] and in flyers, as well as in the church bulletin.

Some church libraries place a box on the return desk labeled "Conscience Fund." Although they have a "no fines" policy, voluntary contributions to ease the conscience may be — and often are — dropped into the box.

Lost books. If a borrower loses a book or reports that a puppy dog has chewed it beyond use, he or she should be expected to pay for it. Ask for the actual price the library paid or for the current list price. Either is reasonable.

Statistics. Keep a count of the items that circulate. An easy way to do this is to count the book cards before they are filed in the circulation file. Weekly records can be cumulated into monthly and annual figures. Mrs. Robert Kennedy of Grand Rapids, Michigan, says, "Numbers mean nothing unless they are posted on a chart which tells a story."[5] Here is an example of the form she uses:

Month:	CIRCULATION RECORDS																					Year:
Week	Classification																					Total
	1	2	3	4	5	6	7	8	9	10	11	12	13	14	15	A	B	C	D	E	F	
1st Week																						
2nd Week																						
3rd Week																						
4th Week																						
5th Week																						
Total																						
Books Acquired	Church Funds:			Gifts:					Memorials:													Total

Classification Code:

1. Fiction	9. Missions	A. Pre-school
2. Lit.,Poetry, Drama	10. Bible. Commentary	B. Primary (grades 1, 2, 3)
3. Inspirational	11. Morals, Ethics	C. Junior (grades 4, 5, 6)
4. Biography	12. Psychology, Education	D. Junior High (grades 7, 8, 9)
5. Devotional	13. Personal Problems, Social	E. Senior High (grades 10, 11, 12)
6. Worship, Music, Art	Welfare	F. Young Adult
7. Church (organization,	14. History, Philosophy,	
denominations)	Religions	
8. Theology, Doctrine	15. Geography, Travel	

Circulation statistics are one index of a library's activity. Report these figures to the official board and to other interested groups and individuals, to help explain how effective the library has been over the year. Make the statistics interesting by comparing the figures to something the audience will understand, such as how many books per family, or per member, were taken out.

Inventory Assets

Plan to inventory the collection from time to time. Normally, a library inventory will be taken every four or five years.

Read the shelves. First, make sure that all books and other materials are in proper sequence on the shelf. This is called "reading" the shelves. It should be done frequently as a standard maintenance procedure, but is especially important before an inventory.

Use the shelf list. The shelf list file is invaluable as an aid in taking the inventory. Not only is it arranged in the same order as the material on the shelf, but it indicates how many copies are in the collection. Remove the rod that holds the cards in the drawer and take the shelf list, one drawer at a time, to the shelves.

Work in pairs. Teamwork speeds up the inventory. One person can read the call number and the copy number from the shelf list card as the other checks the book on the shelf. If the book is on the shelf, place a small pencil check beside the copy number on the card. If it is not, turn the shelf list card on end so the call number is visible.

Inventory snags. Inevitably, there will be snags — differences between what is on the shelf and what is listed in the file. For example:

- A book is on the shelf but no card is in the shelf list file. Remove the book from the shelf. Check the card catalog. If catalog cards are in the file, make up a duplicate shelf list card (marked duplicate) and insert it in the shelf list file. If no catalog cards are in file, decide if you want to keep the book in the collection. If you do, set it aside for cataloging. If not, place it with other material to be discarded. (See Weeding the Collection below.)
- There is a discrepancy between the call number (or copy number) recorded on the book and the shelf list card. Substitute a temporary marker in the shelf list file (with call number and copy number) and remove the original card to be set aside with the book for review and correction later.

Missing items. When inventory of the shelf is completed, check the circulation file for materials that might be in circulation. If a charge-out card is in file, check off the copy on the shelf list card and turn it down in the file. Also check the oversize shelf and special displays. As each item is located, check it off and turn down the card.

After you have looked "everywhere" in the library, some cards might remain standing. Those are the "missing" items.

"Missing" might be a very temporary status, as individuals sometimes take things out of the library fully intending to bring them back "right after class" and do not charge them out. In pencil, therefore, write "missing" with the date and place a marker on the shelf list card before you place it back in file. Every week or so recheck the shelves and all other files to see if the missing items turn up. After a reasonable period of time — perhaps two inventory cycles — the items still missing will be declared lost. (See Withdrawing Material below.) If the book is replaced, it will become copy 2 rather than actually substitute for copy 1. This avoids the confusion that would ensue should the missing copy 1 ever show up again.

Weed the Collection

"Don't be afraid to discard books!" says Juanita Carpenter. "Old books are self-defeating. If there are titles among them that you want for your library, buy new copies. It is so very important that you open your church library with shelves of attractive books that invite browsing and reading."[6]

CSLA Guide on *Selecting Library Materials* offers practical suggestions which are helpful in deciding what to keep and what to discard. (See Resources.) If a book is not taken out of the library or used in two years, chances are it should be withdrawn from the collection to make room for material more in demand.

Helpful hints also can be found in library journals. In one article, for example, Jewel Crocker tells what materials to buy and describes briefly how to clean a book, replace a page or a signature, refasten contents to covers, etc.[7]

Repairs often can be done on a shoestring, using materials "around the house." For example, if a children's book is returned without its cover, make one. Cut two pieces of cardboard slightly larger than the book. Paste colored wrapping paper or wallpaper to the cardboard, extending it around the edges from one side before you paste the other. Make a hinge with mystic tape, leaving just enough room between the cardboards for the spine of the book. Fasten the book into the cover with perforated adhesive cloth or other sturdy tape. An attractive cover illustration can be made from a picture cut from a calendar or magazine. Letter the title on the book cover with magic marker. Add the classification label and your book is ready for circulation again.

Major repairs to hardcover books are more of a challenge. Although some amateurs, with the proper equipment, can turn out a creditable job of rebinding, it often is advisable to select a bookbinder to do the job — or buy a new, fresh copy. Local bookbinders normally are listed in the yellow pages of the telephone directory.

Withdrawing material. Many libraries find it useful to have a small stamp that says "withdrawn." Mark "withdrawn" and the date on (a) the shelf list record, (b) the accession record, and (c) the book itself.

If the withdrawn book is the only copy in your collection, remove the shelf list card and file it in a withdrawn file; pull and destroy all the catalog cards that relate to it. If other copies of the same book are still in the collection, mark "withdrawn" and date after the copy number on the shelf list card and do not remove the catalog cards from file.

To dispose of withdrawn material, hold a used-book sale or donate the items to a church rummage sale or the local thrift shop. Books in good condition, such as unneeded duplicate copies, might be offered to other church libraries. Inner city churches, especially, appreciate such an opportunity.

Withdrawing gift books. What do you do about gifts? Just square your shoulders and discard the gift books that have outlived their usefulness along with the others.

However, if the discarding of gift books — especially memorials — really would be an embarrassment, there are ways to get them off the shelf (if not out of the collection). For example, set up a "Memorials Closet" for the older gift books. Take care, however, that is doesn't become just a dumping place. Make it an asset. Keep it neat and tidy as a showcase to demonstrate how well gift books are regarded. Leave the cards in the card catalog, but mark them to show their new, special location. This way they will still be available, without taking up valuable shelf space needed for the newer, more attractive current materials. Eventually, perhaps, they can be packed and stored away in boxes. In time they may even become archival treasures.

Care and Storage

Give careful thought to the storage and maintenance of all your assets. A well-cared-for collection not only is admired, it is used. And it lasts longer.

Storage. Books are best stored on shelves, lined up side by side and even with the front edge of the shelf — loose enough so they easily can be removed or replaced.

Special media materials often need special storage areas, cabinets, or containers designed for them. For example, the Forcey Memorial Church Library in Washington, D.C., keeps all the audiovisuals in a separate room, but charges them out from the library. These materials include flannelgraphs, flash cards, story strips, song charts, slides, filmstrips and records.[8] Other churches have special files for storing tape cassettes, teaching pictures, and maps. Special storage closets are recommended for equipment such as viewers and screens. See the library supply catalogs for standard library storage containers and other supplies.

Heat, moisture, and careless handling are the enemies of paper and film. Be sure resource materials are not stored near the radiators or in damp places. Try to keep the room temperature regulated. Teach "book etiquette" to minimize turned-down corners, torn pages, and split spines. Offer a projectionist or give personal instruction on use of the equipment to be sure it is handled correctly.

Maintenance. Establish a regular schedule of maintenance that includes dusting and straightening the shelves, as well as cleaning and repairing materials and equipment. Keep the library neat and in order. This encourages respect for the materials, prolongs the life of the resources, and encourages circulation and use.

"A good maintenance program cannot undo damage which has already been done, but it can reduce the likelihood of further damage to existing materials, and markedly increase the life expectancy of new materials," says Pamela W. Darling, head of the Preservation Department, Columbia University Libraries. Pamela says that we have an enormous education job to do, too. "All the skill of the finest restorer can be wasted if the next person to handle the book yanks it across the table by one cover, holds it open with a brick while reading, smashes it down on a copy machine and brings it back to the library in a string bag along with the groceries."[9]

Mending and repair. Library supply houses carry supplies for cleaning and mending library materials. Some of these companies, such as Bro-Dart, Demco and Gaylord, also offer booklets on how to do it. See Library Suppliers.

The repair of audiovisual resources and equipment poses unique problems. Expertise is required. Either learn how to do this from the experts or turn the job over to professional repair people. Much can be learned from talking with librarians who are multimedia specialists, such as most school librarians. Discuss the problems with the dealers or write to the manufacturers for instructions.

Insure the Collection

Insurance is available for many different purposes. Manfred Holck says, "Coverage can actually be secured for almost any desired protection — for a price."[10] Property can be protected under fire, windstorm, hail, explosion, riot, civil commotion, vehicle damage, and damage by smoke, water, heating systems, vandalism or even hazards such as falling trees. Yet the most frequently reported damage to congregational libraries has been from fire, smoke, water, or vandalism.

Determine what should be insured. Estimate the value. Investigate companies and policies, and make sure that any contract signed spells out in detail all the perils that it covers.

Identify assets. Plan to insure anything of value that would need to be replaced in case of loss. This might include resource materials, equipment, and other furnishings in the library.

Make a list. Note the date acquired and the cost, if known. Records maintained for other purposes might well serve as such a list. The following is an example:

"We keep an accession book, but why do we need to maintain a duplicate?" The librarian had a note of exasperation in her voice. This church obviously did not have a photocopying machine and a duplicate meant writing the same information in two copies of the accession book.

"For insurance purposes," answered the church's newly hired administrator. "We need some way to estimate the value of the library in order to determine how much insurance is needed and this record has to be kept in a place away from the library where it will be available for making an insurance claim, if needed." The duplicate copy serves this purpose.

The detailed record of assets can be a photocopy of the accession book, the shelf list file or the accounting records of additions. If the item is a gift, estimate its value. Keep the record current. Most important, keep this insurance record away from the library, preferably in another building. In many cases, the most practical arrangement is to include the library in the insurance policy that covers the parent organization. Adequate insurance may be the best investment you ever make.

Prudent protection. "Faced with mounting losses of material through theft or the nonreturn of books, libraries — large and small — are turning to tougher and more sophisticated security programs," according to a report in *Library Journal.* Electronic security devices are becoming almost mandatory, especially for the protection of rare and valuable material.[11] The average congregational library does not need to adopt such sophisticated measures, but there are sensible steps that can be taken to protect resources and equipment.

Belden Marcus offers the following advice:

(a) Fit exterior building windows, and transoms, if any, with interior key-controlled locks.

(b) Install Underwriters Laboratory approved burglary resistant glass in street-level exterior windows and display windows facing from the library into interior building areaways.

(c) Replace glass pane doors at library area entrances with solid doors.

(d) Install a lock that requires the use of a key from either side of the door. This keeps any intruder from gaining entrance by smashing a glass pane and opening the door by turning an inside bolt.

(e) Place expensive equipment in locked cabinets or closets when not in use.

(f) Maintain outside the library in a secure place a record of the model and serial number of each item.

(g) Place a permanent metal or plastic tag inside each piece of equipment to give the name and location of the congregation.

(h) Encourage the congregation's leadership to make a periodic check for general compliance with local fire codes. Be sure the alarm system includes the library.

(i) Where feasible, avoid placing water sprinklers or soda-acid wet fire extinguishing systems in the library area. Instead, install a dry fire extinguishing system.[12]

Inscribe ownership marks on all materials. In books, stamp the library's name and location on the title page, at least. Example:

MEMORIAL CHURCH LIBRARY
BETHESDA, MARYLAND

On equipment, the identification might be either the above information or a unique identifying number etched or otherwise inscribed on the bottom.

Photograph your valuables. Take a picture of the cover and title page of the most valuable books and the unusual features, such as inscriptions, on equipment. This is useful as proof of ownership should you need to make a claim.

S. Forbes Metcalf says, "Even inexpensive snapshots of your possessions can describe items much more graphically than words, and can provide your insurance company with the proof that is usually needed before reimbursement." Among his suggestions are (a) show valuables and property in their normal settings, (b) start with one wall and move around in a clockwise direction, overlapping each picture slightly so nothing escapes the shutter, (c) when developed, describe each on the back, jotting down prices and purchase dates, if known, (d) put them somewhere safe, away from the location, and (e) update the record periodically.[13]

8

COPING WITH CRISES

"Have you heard?" Marcie's voice over the telephone sounded breathless. "Our church burned to the ground last night!"

The listener could only echo in disbelief, "Not the church!"

"The library and all!"

"Oh, no. How did it happen?"

No one was prepared for the disaster. The beautiful 122-year-old historic structure was in the process of being remodeled, inside and out. The fire started under the eaves of the building and spread throughout. Officials later explained that it was the result of workmen using torches to remove old paint from the outside of the building.[1]

Every library is subject to unexpected crises. Three most frequently reported are fire, theft, and vandalism. What can and should be done to salvage and, possibly, find new opportunities amid the ruins? The following are suggestions taken from the experiences of others.

Fire and Smoke

The First Congregational Church, Wayne, Michigan, reported above, found a "pot of gold at the end of the rainbow." They received a little insurance money and contributions from many members and friends which allowed them to clear the ashes after the fire and rebuild on the site where the old church stood. "We now have a library room many times larger. The wall separating the library from the narthex is done completely with the stained-glass windows that were not destroyed by the fire. The furniture — shelves, reading tables and chairs — is being provided by a family as a living memorial. It now is a very popular room."[2]

Epiphany Episcopal Church, Walpole, Massachusetts, also turned a fire that totally destroyed the library into a "new beginning." They created a Children's Corner in the main building which was spared.

> We started with the idea that any money we had should go towards books so we appealed to members of the parish for help. From them we received a rug, a patchwork quilt, and a number of pillows. In various nooks and crannies of the church we found an old wooden bookcase, a low bench, some child-sized chairs and a low table. Using these items we set to work to create an attractive corner where children could read and look at books as well as choose books to take home.[3]

Pleasant Hill Community Church, Wheaton, Illinois, was struck by lightning. The resultant fire almost destroyed the building, including the church library. Happily, they discovered that the card catalog and a large metal cabinet containing pictures and feltgraphs had been carried out of the building early and were intact. Of their 2,500 book collection, 150 were in circulation. "But the question we had to face immediately was — 'how does one begin again after such a blow?' " the librarian said. "We have since discovered that in many ways there were some blessings in that fire." Among the blessings, she was able to replace an inadequate classification system and adopt the Dewey system. She began by reclassifying the small number of books that had been saved. "Due to the generosity of many friends," she said, "we now have more than 1,000 books with which to begin our new library. The working plans for our new building show a combined library/meeting room approximately twenty-five by thirty feet with an audiovisual storage cabinet. It is located where the traffic will flow by continually."[4]

Bethany Reformed Church, Kalamazoo, Michigan, was able to build new life into its church library after a fire had destroyed the church sanctuary. The fire did not reach the library itself, but the books were affected by the smoke. They dusted the books and packed them in boxes with naphthene flakes to remove the smoke smell. "Shopworn and outdated books were weeded out and discarded. The dirty edges were cleaned by using fine steel wool. The plastic slip cases . . . were cleaned or replaced . . . 800 books were salvaged and these were classified for the first time."[5]

Queens Borough, New York, public library's Woodhaven branch was lost to a fire set by arsonists. "Police say that youngsters entered the building by battering down the rear basement door with timber from a nearby home under reconstruction. Despite the noise caused by the break-in, no one reported the incident. And it was four hours before anyone reported the blaze, which destroyed countless books and records and also damaged office space." A similar fire did extensive damage to the Riddle branch of the Douglas County, Oregon, Library System. The fire was "started by someone who stuffed burning material into the bookdrop" and caused extensive damage.[6]

The University of California has published a 100-page paperback book (1975) called *Managing the Library Fire Risk* by John Morris. It contains photographs and helpful information. Write the author, Room 303, 2118 Milvia Street, Berkeley, CA 94704. Cost is $6.25.

Water Damage

Floods, sprinkler systems, and other sources of water can cause disastrous damage to libraries.

Stanford University had damages caused by a water main break outside the J. Henry Meyer Undergraduate Library. "Water and mud poured into the library basement through holes previously cut for pipes. Water seeped through the basement floor to the sub-basement stacks, where major damage was sustained. . . . Some 40,000 books got waterlogged. . . . The library put out a call for help as thousands of football fans were heading for the stadium. . . . Scores of students, faculty members, and community volunteers flocked to the library to work with Stanford libraries in a race to get the books into cold storage before mold set in. The volunteers wrapped volumes in freezer paper, packed them in cartons, and loaded them (a fork lift truck was made available) into vehicles ranging from rented U-haul vans to a huge refrigerated tractor trailer provided by a local dairy. The cartons were taken to San Jose's Modern Ice Cream Company for freezing." The books were then freeze-dried to restore them.[7]

The Corning Museum of Glass and its library were suddenly faced with catastrophe. "Without warning most of the priceless collection was submerged by flood waters, the aftereffects of a hurricane." Muddy waters had swirled through the library to a depth of more than five feet. The water-logged books expanded and bent the sides of the stacks and were so wedged in that crowbars had to be used to dislodge them. Other shelves sprung their sides and the contents dumped into the mud and water. In the clean-up process, they decided to freeze the books, but there was no electricity, so no freezers. With damage to stores there were no boxes, no paper towels, and no running water for cleaning the mud from the books. They trucked the books to home freezers and commercial freezing lockers 20 to 25 miles away — anyplace where they could be frozen to retard mold growth. Professional help was needed in the restoration process. They decided to replace any book that could be purchased for less than $50. The insurance companies agreed to this program.[8]

In Wyoming, a Disaster Recovery Assistance Team (DRAT) is available to help libraries, archives, historical societies, and other organizations in the state undertake recovery operations to save their materials and buildings from damages associated with fire and flood. More information about DRAT can be obtained by writing Wayne H. Johnson, Wyoming State Library, Cheyenne, WY 82002.[9]

In 1979 the Library of Congress published a second edition of a helpful booklet on *Procedures for Salvage of Water-Damaged Library Materials.* This is available from the Superintendent of Documents, U.S. Government Printing Office, Washington, D.C. 20402.

Theft and Vandalism

A congregation's library is not protected from theft or vandalism just because it is located in a building dedicated to religious causes. These problems no longer are confined to the inner city. With increasing frequency, they occur in the affluent suburbs as well. Careful planning can minimize these dangers.

Vandalism is the result, generally, of impulsive destructive acts. These incidents can be avoided by making it more difficult for intruders to enter. According to Marcus Belden, theft rarely involves the library's books. They are too hard to dispose of for cash. Much more tempting are typewriters, projectors, phonographs, tape recorders, and similar expensive equipment. The measures to discourage vandalism also will discourage entry and theft. In addition to using locks and protective glass, place equipment in locked cabinets or closets when not in use. Maintain outside the library in a secure place a record of the description and model and serial numbers of each of the items. At some inconspicuous spot inside each piece of equipment, affix a metal or plastic tag giving the name and location of the congregation.[10]

Lesser Crises

Perhaps not as dramatic but of equal concern is the discovery of moths, termites, and silverfish, or mold, mildew, and the ravages of age.

Pests. Among common "household" pests are ants, carpet beetles, centipedes, cockroaches, fleas, houseflies, mosquitoes, moths, book lice, silverfish, termites, ticks, spiders, mice and rats, and squirrels. Marguerite Dodd in *America's Homemaking Book* (New York: Charles Scribner's Sons, 1968.) provides line drawings of all these pests, describes their habits, and offers practical steps to eliminate or drive them away. For example, she says book lice like dampness and a dry furnace heat generally will get rid of them; but for a serious infestation use pyrethrum sprays or powder, blown into the crevices of baseboards and window trim. For silverfish, on the other hand, apply a 5 percent residual DDT spray on baseboards, bookcase shelves, in closets, or wherever the silverfish are seen. But don't spray in the cellar if there is a fire in the heater; sprinkle a 10 percent DDT powder instead.

Another helpful booklet, put out by the U.S. Department of Agriculture Science and Education Administration, is Home and Garden Bulletin No. 96, *Controlling Household Pests* (Washington, D.C.: Government Printing Office, July 1979).

Sometimes the only sure way to handle an infestation is to fumigate. Lesser measures just do not do a thorough enough job to eradicate the problem and more drastic measures are needed. Look in the yellow pages of the telephone directory under "Pest Control — Exterminating & Fumigating" for specialists. Find one that offers free estimates and a one-year guarantee. For additional information write the National Pest Control Association, 8150 Leesburg Pike, Vienna, VA 22180.

Mildew. The presence of mold or mildew is unmistakable and can be unpleasant. It is a whitish coating that develops on clothing, furniture, or leather items such as book bindings, and it smells musty. Books stored in a damp basement that has no cross ventilation are certain to develop mildew.

How to prevent it? First, look for clues to the causes. Is there dampness present? Is there excessive humidity in the summer? Samuel Fishlyn recommends that ventilation be improved by installing windows or fans. A dehumidifier will help during the summertime. You may also want to use chloride of lime, suspended in bags.[11]

The librarian of the Huntingdon, Pennsylvania, County Library solved the problem as follows: "At our library we now turn on a few lights in the basement soon after the furnace is no longer needed and let them burn until we start heating in the fall. There has not been a trace of mold since we followed this advice."[12] But how to get rid of it? To rid a room or basement of existing mildew, wash the walls and paneling with bleach or household ammonia. Certain furniture polishes will combat mildew and are safe to use on book bindings. Look for a label which states that the polish can be

)

used for this purpose and apply according to directions. Other products, such as sprays and pellets, are available on the market. These generally are effective as well. Remember to read the label and follow instructions for use.

Newspaper clippings. Helpful hints for preserving or restoring newspaper clippings can often be found in newspaper and magazine articles. For example, a reader asked what could be used on newspaper clippings to keep them from turning yellow. Heloise (copyright King Features Syndicate) gave the following recipe: "There are two ways you might try to preserve those mementos from oblivion. One being to spray them with hair spray (brand name seems to make no difference) lightly three or four times about 30 seconds apart while the clippings are lying on a flat surface. If they have already yellowed, soak them for 10 to 15 minutes, one at a time, in a weak solution of bleach and water. Rinse carefully with clean water and slap them on your refrigerator door to dry."[13]

9

EVALUATING LIBRARY SERVICES

The sky began to darken. We were driving home from work and the view ahead looked threatening. It had rained off and on all day. As we turned onto the high road, it was a surprise to find the sun. The dark clouds and rain were over the river to the left, but the sun shone brightly over the land to the right. Then, like a sudden blessing from above, the rainbows emerged. Not one, but two. Both rainbows were a full array of glorious colors. We exclaimed with excitement and wonder. What a magnificent sight. These certainly were the most beautiful rainbows we had ever seen. What looked like a dreary ride home had turned into a highlight experience.

An evaluation of any situation depends upon the point of view. Some see only the dark clouds and rain. Others catch sight of the rainbow. Still others might be oblivious to both as they ride along in the sun.

When you begin to evaluate library services, admit to yourself that yours is a biased view. You like to believe that the library is wonderful. After all, it's yours. You do have facts to support your view: the number of items added to the collection, how many were borrowed, the number of people who came in on Sunday, etc.

Start with these facts, but don't end there. Try to capture the spirit of the library, the true value of its services to its users.

The reactions of users undoubtedly will reflect differing points of view, but each one is important in assembling the whole picture. A church schoolteacher probably will see the library quite differently from the parishioner who seldom borrows a book. Find out who uses the library and how well it has served their needs. At the same time, try to determine who does not use the library and why.

Refer back to what you set out to accomplish. What were your goals and objectives at the beginning of the year? What were your admitted limitations? What had you hoped to accomplish?

The facts about the collection and its use, the responses of users (or nonusers) to the library and its services, and your own expectations — all these factors together provide the basis for a fair evaluation of a library and its effectiveness.

Reviewing Content and Use

Fact finding comes first. Review the collection to see how it developed during the year. What was added? How much was it used? Then look at the setting. Any changes in location, space, or furnishings? Any changes needed? Consider also the special services that were offered. List them. What did you do to promote the library and its use? Be specific in describing these programs.

Collection development. Each year a number of new resources are selected to be purchased and a number of gifts are received. Most of these items are cataloged so users can find where these materials are located on the shelves. If space is limited, a number of items probably were taken out of the collection. The seldom-used items undoubtedly were withdrawn to make room for current, new materials. A typical balance sheet of assets might read as follows:

Assets Balance Sheet

	Children's Books	Adult Books	Nonbooks	Total
Last year	1,500	2,500	500	4,500
Added				
Gifts	23	75	0	
Purchases	150	200	55	
Total	173	275	55	503

Withdrawn	15	25	2	42
Total	1,658	2,750	553	4,961

Often there is a story behind the numbers that will make them more interesting. For example, library users of the Central Methodist Church, Lansing, Michigan, were encouraged to submit recommendations for purchase. Then, the library committee met twice a year to consider and select additions. The library reported, "an effort is made to select books which will interest the patrons, from small children through adults, in areas including the Bible, history, nature, fiction, missions, the family, and worship."[1] Such an explanation makes the numbers more meaningful.

Use of resources. Administrators like to know that an investment is paying off. So be sure to count the number of items in the library that have been used during the past year. Example:

Circulation	Last year	This year
Books	1,200	1,800
Nonbooks	120	180
Equipment	60	90

Enhance these figures with additional information. For example, note that the number of books taken out last year averaged one per member (or four per family); and that the circulation of nonbooks, audiovisuals, and other materials increased by 33 percent (or by one-third). If use has gone down, find out why. There must be an explanation.

Identify special collections, such as the reference books, or materials set aside for the mission study, the summer reading club, or special holidays. Count how many items were borrowed after a list was inserted in the Sunday bulletin or posted on a bulletin board in the hallway. This demonstrates results.

Special services. Describe any activities that resulted in greater use of the library and its resources during the year. This might include visits to classes or class visits to the library, visits to shut-ins, story hours, book reviews, or operation of equipment for class sessions.

Promotion. Include promotional activities in your evaluation, although they might not be easy to measure. These include book displays, posters, or booklets on how to use the library.

Space and facilities. Think about your library's setting. Is its location easy to get to and the arrangement of materials easy to use? Anything new this year?

If the location has changed, or if the library has expanded into an adjoining room, or if furnishings have been rearranged to create a more relaxed reading area, that's progress. But if nothing has changed and the space needs reported last year have not been met, this also is worthy of note. If the need is critical, be prepared to explain why.

Staffing. How many hours of volunteer time was spent on preparing materials for use or helping users in the library? How many individuals took part in these library activities? What library workshops and conferences were attended so the staff would be more able to serve efficiently? The loyal service of the library committee and staff is important to library use. Recognize this as a vital contribution.

Getting Feedback from Users

With the above information, you know what your library has to offer. The next step is to find out how it is being received. What do patrons think of your library? What is its value to them?

Unsolicited response. Comments from library users are an indication. Recently a church schoolteacher came into the library looking for specific books. The staff member on duty helped her to find them. Her comment: "This library is a lot better than it used to be. Oh, it has always been good, but now you have so many new materials that we need."

"An important component of evaluations," says Jane Ann Hannigan, Associate Professor in the School of Library Science at Columbia University, "is also the response given by a child. . . . Children giggling, laughing, or crying as they follow some tall tale or pursue a magical beast. . . . We have yet to design the means to measure what children take out of the system." She suggests that we develop a keener and more precise sense of observation in our daily encounters with users.[2]

The survey. A more formal means of gathering feedback is a survey. Develop a simple questionnaire. Give a copy to each user of the library, distribute copies at entryways to the church, or insert it in the Sunday bulletin. A one-page multiple-choice question sheet can determine how many people actually use the library, how often they use it, and what they think of its service.

The librarian of the Mohr, Rhode Island, Library decided to find out the pattern of public library use. "Caught unprepared when last winter's fuel shortage curtailed schools' field trips to the library, we decided to take survey materials and a slide show of the library's services to the schools." The slides were presented before the survey was distributed. Even though some may be familiar with the library, they probably will not remember everything.[3]

The survey might include questions about any or all of the following:

- Browsing accessibility of library materials
- Usefulness of the card catalog
- Reading or reference assistance from staff
- Instructions in use of materials or equipment
- Adequacy of facilities for reading, viewing, or listening
- Availability of materials for borrowing (or interlibrary loan)
- Working place for preparation of AV's, posters, etc.
- Storytelling, book reviewing, service to shut-ins, etc.
- Special collections
- Cooperative support of programs, such as special displays, etc.

Measuring Achievement

The facts gathered from the librarian along with the subjective responses from the users (and nonusers) form the basis for a fairly objective evaluation. Add to this the opinions of others outside the congregation.

Outside recognition. The Fourth Presbyterian Church in Bethesda asked an outside consultant to evaluate their media center and make recommendations. The result helped them make the decision to hire a full-time librarian instead of a part-time one.

Awards recognize the library's worth in the larger community. Each year the Church and Synagogue Library Association honors outstanding congregational libraries and librarians. In 1981, the following CSLA awards were presented: Outstanding Congregational Library, Lutheran Church of the Holy Comforter, Baltimore; Outstanding Congregational Librarian, Margaret Taylor, First Baptist Church, Warren, Ohio; Outstanding Contribution to Librarianship, Library Committee, Central Presbyterian Church, Terre Haute, Indiana; and the Helen Keating Ott Award for children's literature to Phyllis A. Wood, South San Francisco.

Standards. The CSLA Guide No. 6 on *Standards for Church and Synagogue Libraries* (Bryn Mawr, Pennsylvania: Church and Synagogue Library Association, 1977) provides guidelines for measuring effectiveness and progress. CSLA also publishes a bimonthly bulletin, *Church & Synagogue Libraries*, which includes information about effective libraries.

Read up about other libraries and visit as many as you can. How does yours measure up to others of similar size and potential? Remember that each library has its own objectives, as well as constraints and unique advantages.

Specific programs. A fair way to measure progress is to determine if you met the objectives you established at the beginning of the year. Look at each of the programs, with their projected timetable, requirements, and costs. How well did you do? Did you accomplish what you set out to do? Don't be afraid to admit that a specific objective was not met. Explain why. Perhaps another objective took priority? Perhaps costs rose more sharply than expected? Say so. This helps to determine what still needs to be done.

Reporting to the Administration

A summary of library activities and progress should be reported to the sponsor(s) annually at least. A sponsor is the person to whom you report (the next step up in the organization chart) or anyone who provides support in the way of funding (such as the women's society). Cultivate this channel of communication.

Annual report. This yearly summary serves more than one purpose. It keeps the administration informed. When presented before budget time, it is a reminder that the library is effective but has continuing need for support. Finally, it is the springboard for establishing objectives and planning programs for the year ahead.

Include a statistical summary, facts about the collection and its use, and examples of events or services that have been effective.

Oral reports. Make it a habit to get your library onto the agenda of important meetings, such as the Administrative Board. This provides an opportunity to present short reports of current library activities and successes.

"Librarians by nature are not salespersons, but selling is one of their most important jobs," says James Swan, director of the Pickens County Library in Easley, South Carolina. He suggests the following:

- See things from the users' point of view.
- Build on the strengths of present successful programs.
- Brainstorm with the staff.
- Emphasize any special services you have.
- Let groups know you are available for a program—even on a moment's notice.
- Reach people where they are and where they congregate.

"Visibility," Swan says, "is the name of the game."[4]

10

PLANNING FOR THE FUTURE

Life is a series of new beginnings that rise out of dreams and aspirations. Each new season begins with hopes high and energies renewed.

Weeks ahead of the disappearance of snow and cold, we begin looking through seed catalogs. The color pictures of flowers and vegetables are enticing. Although some of our yard is too shady for most annuals, careful planning and selection usually yield something to enliven the garden all summer. Each year as each new shoot breaks through the ground, our hopes and expectations rise.

One year, however, our mail order from the catalog produced mixed results. Some of the small bulbs just would not sprout. After an initial spurt of new growth, the spruce tree seedlings died. The pink roses that we had ordered turned out to be red. Nevertheless, the red roses were beautiful, accenting the blue hydrangia bushes already there, and the dahlias were unexpectedly gorgeous in bloom.

Careful planning had been given to what already was there, what the conditions were for growth, and what was needed to fulfill our dreams of a summer garden. The end result was not quite what we planned, but rewards often come with unplanned developments. So it is with planning library services. Each year the planning, the hopes, the expectations begin anew.

Beginning Again

Begin each season by reviewing your basic purposes and how far along you have come in supporting these. Plan for the coming year, with objectives that really can be reached within that time limit. Sometimes a program fails because it is based on unrealistic expectations. Be honest about what reasonably can be achieved. But don't lose that sense of adventure, that optimistic enthusiasm, which is necessary for development and growth.

With your annual report in hand, you know what assets you have, how successful your services have been, and what still needs to be done to support long-range goals. CSLA Guide No. 1, *Setting Up a Library; How To Begin or Begin Again*, presents a planning outline based on ten action steps that take you from beginning-with-a-purpose to stretching-your-horizons. See Resources.

Setting New Goals

Think big. Have lofty long-range goals. Each year, tackle what reasonably can be done toward reaching those goals. Annual objectives provide the framework for planning the library's programs for the year ahead.

Brainstorm. Get everyone involved in the planning. Begin with a brainstorming session with your library staff and with key people who are major users of the library. Decide together what needs to be done and what the priorities should be.

Programs and projects. Some programs will be continuous; they will be included in the planning year after year. Examples of these are the acquisition of materials, cataloging, etc. Begin with these. Then add other programs that are needed this year, such as a used-book sale to dispose of materials taken out of the collection. Conclude with programs that it would be nice to have, such as preparation of book displays each Sunday to enhance the sermon.

Participating in Cooperative Ventures

Librarians are finding that there are cost savings in cooperative processing and that services can be expanded when they
share resources with other libraries in a network.

Cooperative processing. Discounts can be higher for quantity purchases. Try pooling purchases of supplies and other
materials with other librarians in your community.

One church librarian in Silver Spring, Maryland, purchased a number of rolls of clear plastic to cover paperback
books. Through an interdenominational fellowship group she
offered other church librarians single rolls for purchase. They
all benefited from the quantity purchase price.

Thomas H. Nankervis reports, "Small clusters of churches
in Nebraska (belonging to the Missouri Synod Lutheran
Church) and California (basically Presbyterian) have entered
into a cooperative arrangement to purchase such expensive
items as 16-mm films. The idea of one church listing resources that belong to another church or several churches
working together to purchase materials is not 'far-fetched'; it
is good stewardship."[1]

Even cataloging can be more fun in a "cataloging bee."
Choose a central location. Share the cost of the reference
tools needed in cataloging. Consider developing a union list
of the holdings of participating libraries, and take advantage
of being able to copy the information if someone else has
already cataloged the item.

Share use of materials. Many librarians will allow books
and other materials to be borrowed on interlibrary loan. Our
Bethesda Methodist Church once borrowed a group of books
from the local public library for use during the Vacation
Bible School. In turn, we loaned some books to another church
library that was just getting started.

If you are willing to let outsiders use your library, make
this fact known. Tell the public librarian that nonmembers
are welcome to use your reference collection, by appoint-
ment or when the library normally is open and staffed.

Fellowship groups. Get to know other people who are work-

ing in church and synagogue libraries. Discover that by working together you can have better libraries and greater
resource potential. Teach and learn and share in an interdenominational fellowship. Pool your resources and ideas. Benefit
from the training, experience and diversified resources in
other libraries.

Keeping Up with Trends

Change is inevitable. Over a period of time you might find
that the character of the congregation you serve has changed,
or new techniques and services have suddenly become available within the reach of smaller libraries. Be attuned to your
environment in planning for the future. Keep up with the
trends.

User community. At the time our library began, the congregation was a good mix of young and old parishioners. By the
time our library was seven years old, three new churches had
been established in the rapidly growing suburbs and began
attracting some of our members, frequently the younger families who lived in those suburbs. Then, in its second ten
years, the library grew older and so did the congregation. A
greater percentage of middle-aged and senior parishioners
filled the pews. At the same time, the Methodist Church
merged with the Church of the Brethren, to become the United
Methodist Church. This brought other changes. Adjustments
were made in the organization of work areas, in programs,
and in resource materials.[2]

The needs and interests of a user community can and do
change—whether gradually or abruptly. Be prepared for this.
Be responsive. Keep your library plans flexible enough to
adapt to change as you go along.

Information community. Libraries in the broader community are changing too. Exciting things are happening. A few
years ago the lead article in the *Wall Street Journal* observed
that libraries are no longer just places to come in out of the
rain. The public hunger for knowledge has never been greater, and the school or town library of today is apt to be a

bustling place, not a deserted one. "To help meet this strain on their facilities, librarians are experimenting, innovating." They are using high-speed, teletypewriters (to borrow from other libraries), computerizing their libraries, demanding funding, and participating in cooperative programs with other libraries.[3]

Libraries are giving better service through a diversity of materials and advanced technologies. Many congregational libraries have become multimedia resource centers, with greater emphasis on materials such as films, videotapes, sound recordings, listening stations, games, kits, and other interesting new media forms.

Betty Fast, director of media services for the Groton, Connecticut, public schools says, "Media programs are vital in education because of the great changes in the learning patterns of youngsters, caused largely by their exposure to television and other mass media."[4]

Today's libraries must be in the middle of the action. They must provide the kind of information that will satisfy individual needs and help solve people problems. They must use modern techniques to catch attention, hold interest, and transfer information efficiently and effectively to the people.

Some churches now use their own equipment to videotape special programs or to train teachers and speakers. Videotapes of programs are available for loan from many public libraries.

The Public Television Library (475 L'Enfant Plaza SW, Washington, D.C. 20024) permits subscribers to borrow video programs on 3/4" U-matic and has 350 titles in the subject areas of health, science, public affairs, creative and performing arts and how-to's. Fotomat outlets, seen in many parking lots and street corners, will convert 8-mm film to Betamax or VHS videocassettes for a nominal fee. These and similar bits of information about this rapidly growing field can be found in *Cable Libraries*, issued monthly by C. S. Tepfer Publishing Co., Inc. (Box 565, Ridgefield, CT 06877).

Church Resource Systems (P.O. Box 990, Dallas, TX 75221) operates the Membership Services, Inc. (MSI), which provides automated record management systems for more than 400 churches of many faiths from California to Florida. They offer systems for managing membership, stewardship, prospects, bookkeeping, mailing of envelopes, and the music library.

Media specialists say, "New technology will be a part of the future, whether the school is in Texas or Georgia."[5]

Anticipate the future. The following trends are likely to continue: growing diversity of materials and services, resource sharing through formal and informal networks, and advances in technologies, such as microcomputers and video recording. The library will emerge as a new kind of service center.

In the church or synagogue, the library will become a learning, information, and communications center—bringing together the activities of communications, education, library information, and records management. These functions will work together quite naturally as they will use the same communications techniques, equipment, and space. This center will be a meeting place, a processing facility, and an information resource.

Emphasis will be away from programs, as such, and more toward meeting the needs of individual persons for information, communication, learning, sharing ideas with others, and even entertainment (which can communicate a message of hope or inspiration).[6]

One last bit of advice: Try not to be impatient or discouraged if others do not have the same vision as you. Retain that enthusiasm and confidence with which you began. Remember that big hopes and dreams come from God. Be willing to let go and let him lead. With God as your partner, good things just naturally will follow.

NOTES

Chapter 1

1. "Washington Hebrew Congregation, Washington, D.C." by Alice F. Toomey. *Church & Synagogue Libraries*, 3:11, January 1970.
2. "Carl Weller, Book Selector, Reads for a Living" by Kathryn Ericson. *Lutheran Libraries*, 19:78, Fall 1977.

Chapter 2

1. *With No Fear of Failure* by Tom J. Fatjo, Jr. and Keith Miller. Waco, TX: Word Books, 1981.

Chapter 3

1. "How to Finance a Church or Synagogue Library" by Betty McMichael. *Church & Synagogue Libraries* 11:1, November/December 1977.
2. "Library Memorials" by Rose C. Wolf. *Library Journal* 103:1546, September 1, 1978.
3. "Sound Policies, Good Leaders Mean ... A Successful Library in New Mexico" by Rev. Donald L. Campbell. *Church & Synagogue Libraries* 12:4–5 September/October 1978.
4. "Hard Work and Love Bring Library New Life" *Church & Synagogue Libraries* 9:1, 3 November/December 1975.
5. "Memorial Honors Library Worker" *Church & Synagogue Libraries* 9:3 January/February 1976.
6. "Librarian Gives Library as Memorial" *Lutheran Libraries* 7:15 Winter 1964.
7. "Used Books Are Dollar Stretchers" by Lillian S. Kaiser. *Church & Synagogue Libraries*, 12:1, September/October 1978.
8. "How to Finance a Church or Synagogue Library" by Betty McMichael. *Church & Synagogue Libraries*, 11:1, 12, November/December 1977.
9. "Need Money? Try Borrowing" *Church & Synagogue Libraries* 11:7 May/June 1978.

10. "Plan a Fund-Raiser That Really Make$ Money" *Changing Times* 30:33–34 February 1976.
11. "10 Ideas for Raising Money for Your Club" by Sandy Kimball. *Retirement Living*, 16:26–28, March 1976.
12. "How to Raise Money for a Good Cause and Have a Good Time Doing It" by Sandra Oddo. *House & Garden*, 148:145–146, November 1976.

Chapter 4

1. "Professor Defends Live-in Chicken Coop" by Conan Putnam. *The Washington Star*, October 16, 1978.
2. "Washington Hebrew Congregation, Washington, D.C." by Alice F. Toomey. *Church & Synagogue Libraries* 3:11–12 January 1970.
3. "Annual Award - 1970; Presented to Mrs. Helen Dempsey of Birmingham, Michigan" *Church & Synagogue Libraries* 3:4 July 1970.
4. "Blueprint for a Church Library at Gethsemane of Hopkins, Minn." by Peg Gardner. *Lutheran Libraries* 5:3 Fall 1962.
5. "Convert Your Sunday School; Become a Lunar-Age Multimedia Learning Center" by Richard M. Morris. *Church & Synagogue Libraries* 6:1 July-August 1973.
6. *Planning and Furnishing the Church Library* by Marian S. Johnson. Minneapolis, MN: Augsburg Publishing House, 1966.
7. "This Way Out — From Our Mad Jumble of Signs" by Wolf Von Eckardt. *IEEE Transactions on Professional Communication* PC-21:63 June 1978.
8. "Bus Tour Provides Ideas, Fellowship and Nature's Beauties" by Joanne Jensen. *Lutheran Libraries* 19:4 Winter 1976.
9. "Library Front-Liners — Kenneth H. Sayers: YA Librarian With a Do-It-Yourself Flair" *Wilson Library Bulletin* 49:344–345 January 1975.
10. "Libraries: Not Just Books" by John J. Kurtz. *The Washington Post*, November 24, 1977.
11. *Catholic Library Practice*, edited by Brother David Mar-

tin. Vol. 2. Portland, OR: University of Portland Press, 1950.

12. "Furniture for Fingertip Access" *Church & Synagogue Libraries* 5:6-7 January-February 1972.

13. "Ideas for Children's Book Shelves" *Lutheran Libraries* 18:78 Fall 1976.

14. "The Church Library Aids the Parish Program" by Edith Maxfield. *The Christian Educator*, 9:3-4, 29, July-September 1966.

15. "A 'Do It Yourself' Periodical Shelf" by Bette Caum Royal. *Church and Synagogue Libraries* 4:9 July 1971.

16. "Pillows, Quilts and Soapboxes" *School Library Journal* 22:31 February 1976.

17. "LCLA Chapter News—Milwaukee Chapter" by Lorraine Pike. *Lutheran Libraries* 20:9 Winter 1977.

18. "A Pre-School Child's Visit to the Library" by Violet M. Neger. *Church & Synagogue Libraries* 8:1,12 January /February.

Chapter 5

1. "An Alternative to Library School" by Westwell R. Daniels. *Library Journal*, 103:1702, September 15, 1978.

2. "Love It or Leave It" by Mary Eble. *Wilson Library Bulletin* 49:385 January 1975.

3. "A Labor of Love" by Lee Kelly. *Church & Synagogue Libraries* 8:9 May-June 1975.

4. "Volunteers? Yes!" by Elfrieda McCauley. *School Library Journal*, 22:29, May 1976.

5. *The Seven Worlds of the Minister* by Gerald Kennedy. New York: Harper & Row, 1968.

6. "Special Report—Volunteers in Libraries" *Library Journal* 101:2431-2 December 1, 1976.

7. "The Organization and Operation of a Church Library" by June B. and Earl E. Dorn. *Church & Synagogue Libraries* 7:3-5 November/December 1973.

8. "The Library, First Lutheran Church, Ellicott City, Maryland" by Mrs. Herbert M. Payne. *Church & Synagogue Libraries* 3:7 May 1970.

9. "Responsibilities of Librarianship" by Sarah L. Wallace. *Church & Synagogue Libraries* 5:1–2, 6–7 July-August 1972.
10. "Thirteen Steps to Library Orientation" by Betty Kouns. *School Library Journal*, 23:125, March 1977.
11. "CSLA News—Delaware Valley Chapter" *Church & Synagogue Libraries*, 10:5, May-June 1977.
12. "Utah Offers Correspondence Course for Church, Synagogue Librarians." *Church & Synagogue Libraries* 11:1, 3 September/October 1977.
13. "CSLA News - News of the Congregational Library World." *Church & Synagogue Libraries* 11:3 May-June 1978.
14. "CSLA News - News of the Congregational Library World." *Church & Synagogue Libraries* 11:3 March/April 1978.
15. "Church Library Course" *Church & Synagogue Libraries* 11:3 May-June 1978.

Chapter 6

1. *Church Business Policies Outlined* by Eugene C. Neithold. Greenville, SC: Church Books, 1976.
2. *Audio-Visual Materials in the Church Library; How to Select, Catalog, Process, Store, Circulate, and Promote* by Margaret Barton Korty. Church Library Council, 5406 Quintana Street, Riverdale, MD 20840, 1977.
3. *CRS Update*, vol. 6, Fall 1979.
4. "The Audiovisual Supplier: Dealing With Dealers and Distributors" by Edward J. Hingers. *Library Trends*, 24: 737 April 1976.
5. "Do Publishers and Librarians Mix?" by William Gentz. *Church & Synagogue Libraries*, 4:1–2, May 1971.
6. "Libraries: Not Just Books" by John J. Kurtz. *The Washington Post*, Md. 5, November 4, 1977.
7. "Hennepin Wins Award for Drug Film Program." *American Libraries* 10:626, November 1979.
8. "Videotape Circulation Burgeons" *American Libraries*, 10:438, July/August 1979.
9. "AV Services: Frills No Longer" by Maxine Jones. *American Libraries*, 10:555, October 1979.

10. "Added Entries" by Jacqulyn Anderson. *Media; Library Services Journal*, 9:34–35, April, May, June 1979.
11. Public Law 94-553, "Copyrights Act," October 19, 1976.
12. "Cassettes—The Simple, Inexpensive Things You Can Do With Them and the More Complicated Things, Too" by J. Kevin Dougherty, Instructional Materials Coordinator, White Plains (NY) High School, speaking at the 13th Annual Conference of the Church and Synagogue Library Association, June 30, 1980, West Hartford, CT.

Chapter 7

1. *Church Business Policies Outlined* by Eugene C. Neithold. Greenville, SC: Church Books, 1976.
2. "Church Budgets for Part-Time Librarian" *Church & Synagogue Libraries*, 4:8, March 1971.
3. "Nickel Victories - II" by John Berry. *Library Journal* 101:2105, October 15, 1976.
4. "There is an Alternative to Fines" by Jack W. Griffith. *School Library Journal*, 23:50, April 1977.
5. "Reader Suggests Forms for Circulation Records" *Lutheran Libraries*, Fall 1963.
6. "Libraries Need Weeding and Feeding" by Juanita Carpenter. *Lutheran Libraries*, 17:55, Summer 1975.
7. "Care and Repair of Books" by Jewel Crocker. *Church & Synagogue Libraries*, 6:5–6, January-February 1973.
8. "Forcey Memorial Church Library" *Church Library Council News* (National Capital and Suburban Areas), Fall 1979.
9. "A Local Preservation Program: Where to Start" by Pamela W. Darling. *Library Journal*, 101:2343, November 15, 1976.
10. *Money Management for Ministers* by Manfred Holck, Jr. Minneapolis, MN: Augsburg Publishing House, 1966.
11. "Security in Libraries" 104:878, April 15, 1979.
12. "Safeguarding the Library and Its Collection" by Belden Marcus. *Church & Synagogue Libraries*, 5:3, March-April 1972.
13. "Photographing Your Valuables for Insurance or Tax Pur-

poses" by S. Forbes Metcalf. *Retirement Living*, 16:44–5, January 1976.

Chapter 8

1. "Portrait of a Church" by Marcella Maas. *Church & Synagogue Libraries*, 8:6–7, July-August 1975.
2. "Portrait of a Church" by Marcella Maas. *Church & Synagogue Libraries*, 8:6–7, July-August 1975.
3. "Out of a Fire—A Children's Corner" by Mrs. Stanton E. Gull, Jr. *Church & Synagogue Libraries*, 10:2, 16, July/August 1977.
4. "Illinois Library Destroyed by Fire Finds New Purpose" by Nancy Dick. *Church & Synagogue Libraries*, 13:8, September/October 1979.
5. "Fire in Kalamazoo Responsible for Reactivation of a Church Library" by Marie Karman Morgan. *Church & Synagogue Libraries* 7:1–2, March/April 1974.
6. "Arsonists Hit Libraries in New York and Oregon" *Library Journal*, 103:1552, September 1, 1978.
7. "Water Main Break at Stanford Damages 40,000 Books" *Library Journal*, 103:2468, December 15, 1978.
8. "Resuscitating a Water-logged Library" by John H. Martin. *Wilson Library Bulletin*, 50:233–241, November 1975.
9. "DRAT Emergency Team To Help Out in Wyoming" *Library Journal*, 104:2504–6, December 1, 1979.
10. "Safeguarding the Library and Its Collection" by Marcus Belden. *Church & Synagogue Libraries*, 5:3, March-April 1972.
11. "Mildew Moves" by Samuel Fishlyn. *The Washington Post*, p. E-27, October 20, 1979.
12. "Mold Again" *Gaylords' Triangle* (Gaylord Bros, Inc.), 44:2, October 1964.
13. "Hints from Heloise" *The Washington Star*, November 11, 1978.

Chapter 9

1. "The Church Library in Action" by Lenora M. Sykes and

Mary Armstrong. *International Journal of Religious Education*, 40:22, October 1963.

2. "Evaluation as a Search for Value" by Jane Ann Hannigan. *School Library Journal*, 23:24–25, September 1976.

3. "Who's Not Using the Library? Survey Students" *School Library Journal*, 21:29, January 1975.

4. "New Visibility for the Small Public Library" by James Swan. *Wilson Library Bulletin*, 51:424–427, January 1977.

Chapter 10

1. "More than Bookshelves" by Thomas H. Nankervis. *Church & Synagogue Libraries*, 6:5–7, March-April 1973.

2. "The Bethesda United Methodist Church Library" by Ruth S. Smith. In *Church and Synagogue Libraries*. Ed. by John F. Harvey. Metuchen, NJ: Scarecrow Press, 1980, pp. 206–8.

3. "Modern Libraries/Federal Aid Will Speed Addition of Materials, Improvement of Service/Teletypewriter Links Locate Books in California; Use of Magnetic Tapes to Rise/ Librarians Shatter the Silence" by Ronald G. Shafer. *The Wall Street Journal*, November 1, 1975.

4. "The Media Specialist as an Agent for Change" by Betty Fast. *Wilson Library Bulletin*, 49:636, May 1975.

5. "Priorities for Rounding Out a Century" by Mary Kingsbury. *Wilson Library Bulletin*, 50:398, January 1976.

6. "In Cataloging and Networks ... What's New in the Library World?" by Ruth S. Smith. *Church & Synagogue Libraries*, 13:1, 4–5, September-October 1979.

Resources

The following books and pamphlets have proved to be helpful to churches and synagogues in organizing and operating library services for the congregation. They are available from the Church and Synagogue Library Association, P.O. Box 1130, Bryn Mawr, PA, 19010. Various denominations and commercial sources also offer helpful guides.

CSLA Guide Series

CSLA Guide No. 1
   Setting Up a Library; How to Begin or Begin Again, by Ruth
   S. Smith. 1979.
CSLA Guide No. 2 (Rev. 2nd ed.)
   Promotion Planning All Year 'Round, by Claudia Han-
   naford and Ruth S. Smith. 1978.
CSLA Guide No. 3 (Rev. ed.)
   Workshop Planning, by Ruth S. Smith. 1979.
CSLA Guide No. 4 (Rev. ed.)
   Selecting Library Materials, by Arthur W. Swarthout. 1978.
CSLA Guide No. 5
   Cataloging Books Step By Step, by Ruth S. Smith. 1977.
CSLA Guide No. 6
   Standards For Church and Synagogue Libraries. 1977.
CSLA Guide No. 7
   Classifying Church or Synagogue Library Materials, by Dor-
   othy B. Kersten. 1977.
CSLA Guide No. 8
   Subject Headings for Church or Synagogue Libraries, by
   Dorothy B. Kersten. 1978.
CSLA Guide No. 9
   *A Policy and Procedure Manual for Church and Synagogue
   Libraries*, by Martin Ruoss. 1980.
CSLA Guide No. 10
   Archives in the Church or Synagogue Library, by Evelyn R.
   Ling. 1981.

CSLA Bibliographies

A Basic Book List for Church Libraries, by Bernard E. Deitrick.
   Rev. ed. 1979.
Church and Synagogue Library Resources, by Rachel Kohl
   and Dorothy Rodda. 3rd ed. 1979.

Other Publications

*Cataloging Made Easy; How To Organize Your Congrega-
   tion's Library*, by Ruth S. Smith. New York: The Seabury
   Press, 1978. 263p.
*Getting the Books Off the Shelves; Making the Most of Your
   Congregation's Library*, by Ruth S. Smith. New York: The
   Seabury Press, 1979. 128p.

Library Associations and Denominational Groups

The following library associations and denominational groups offer church and/or synagogue library services. A more complete list can be found in CSLA Bibliography on *Church and Synagogue Library Resources* and in an article by William H. Gentz, one of the founders of the Lutheran Church Library Association and a former president of the Church and Synagogue Library Association, on "Church and Synagogue Libraries Make Up an Expanding Market" in *Publishers Weekly,* September 21, 1978.

Association of Jewish
  Libraries
Synagogue Division
c/o National Foundation for
  Jewish Culture
122 East 42 Street
New York, NY 10017

Catholic Library Association
Parish and Community
  Library Section
461 Lancaster Avenue
Haverford, PA 19041

Church and Synagogue
  Library Association
Box 1130
Bryn Mawr, PA 19010

Church Library Department
Southern Baptist
  Convention
127 Ninth Avenue North
Nashville, TN 37234

Cokesbury Church Library
  Association
201 Eighth Avenue South,
  Room 248
Nashville, TN 37202

Evangelical Church Library
  Association
P.O. Box 353
Glen Ellyn, IL 60137

Lutheran Church Library
  Association
122 West Franklin Avenue
Minneapolis, MN 55404

Library Supply Houses

The following is a selected list. Additional names can be found in indexes available in most public libraries and in the September 1 issue of *Library Journal* which includes an "Annual Buyers' Guide."

Bro-Dart, Inc.
Box 3037
1649 Memorial Avenue
Williamsport, PA 17705

Demco Educational Corp.
Box 7488
Madison, WI 53707

Gaylord Brothers
Library Supplies &
    Equipment
Box 4901
Syracuse, NY 13221

Highsmith Company, Inc.
Box 25
Highway 106 East
Fort Atkinson, WI 53538

Library Bureau
Mohawk Valley Community
    Corp.
801 Park Avenue
Herkimer, NY 13357